"It has become clearer to me than ever that my personal relationship with Jesus is the heart of my existence as a believer. Of the many devotionals I've read over the 50 years I've followed Jesus, this one centers most on Jesus. If you want a deeper walk with the One who washed us from our sins in His own blood, this is the devotional for you."

-Ed Underwood, former pastor of the historic Church of the Open Door and author of When God Breaks Your Heart, Reborn to be Wild, and the Trail.

"As a recovering people-pleaser myself, I found this devotional by Richter to be a refreshing guide to prayer and a deeper peace with Jesus."

-Mary E. Twomey, author of the Undraland series

Prayer: a Conversation with Jesus

Renee Richter

WESTBOW
PRESS®
A DIVISION OF THOMAS NELSON
& ZONDERVAN

WestBow Press books may be ordered through booksellers or by contacting:

WestBow Press
A Division of Thomas Nelson & Zondervan
1663 Liberty Drive
Bloomington, IN 47403
www.westbowpress.com
1 (866) 928-1240

ISBN: 978-1-9736-8119-9 (sc)
ISBN: 978-1-9736-8120-5 (hc)
ISBN: 978-1-9736-8118-2 (e)

Library of Congress Control Number: 2019920144

Print information available on the last page.

WestBow Press rev. date: 12/27/2019

Contents

This book is a thank-you to two dear friends who led me on a journey to discover Jesus through prayer. I dedicate this book to them:

Angela Jaqua, who lives out her friendship with Jesus in front of anyone who listens or takes a moment to see the light of Jesus emanating from her, no matter what her circumstance. Dear sister, you have taught more than you can know, despite my efforts to tell you.

Liz Ciaravino, who partnered with me on a journey to discover Jesus more deeply and showed me intercessory and listening prayer. Prayer isn't just about my words to Jesus; it's about listening for the direction of the Holy Spirit as I join Him to pray for those in need. Prayer became a partnership. Liz, thank you for giving your time to me as we journeyed together with Jesus.

This is also for those who open these pages and take the time to read and ponder the words. Prayer and a relationship with Jesus aren't for an elite, specially selected group of people. Prayer is for each of us, knit in the womb by Jesus Himself. He took the time to design each of us. Why wouldn't He take the time to listen to each of us?

Revelation 5:8 tells us there are golden bowls, filled with the prayers of the saints, placed next to the throne of God. He breathes these prayers in as incense. This is how precious our prayers are to Him. They have a place next to the throne of God and He breathes them in, making them a part of Himself.

Acknowledgments

How do I thank all those who have taken part in this book? Many have prayed, listened to entries, read entries, edited, and just encouraged me along the way—too many to thank individually. I have been blessed and encouraged by every one of them. I know that their faithfulness to our Lord Jesus Christ and me has been a tremendous benefit to the completion of this book and all that will be accomplished in the hearts of those who read this and find Jesus in prayer.

How do I effectively thank the man who has stood by my side for the last thirty-one–plus years? He has been my constant support and encouragement through this entire journey. Bruce picked up those things that got left undone or were too hard to finish while I was completing this project. He has encouraged me when I get overwhelmed and has prayed along with me for this endeavor and what Jesus has done and will continue to do. It's incredible to have all of the support and love he so generously gives me.

My daughter, Jessica, also an aspiring author, was often a phone call or text away and shared in the joy of much of this book. Writers have a special appreciation for the efforts of writing early in the morning and late into the night. It's such a blessing to have someone who gets the process, the passion, and the joy.

My niece Danika Delello has put much time and dedication into this book. She helped with the title and the initial editing and making sure the message of my heart was conveyed clearly on the page. What a pleasure to share this special blessing with you.

Thank you to all of you from the bottom of my heart.

Foreword

I have known Renee since I was a young teenager, and now I have a few young teenagers. In the many years, I have known Renee, I have always been so impressed with her deep and genuine relationship with Jesus. You know how there are some people that talk about God, and it's clear they know a lot about Him? Then there are others who when they talk about God, it's clear that they actually know Him, not just *about* Him. The truth is that the only reason there is a difference is that some people settle to only know about God even though His invitation is to know Him. I grew up in the church since I can remember and I've been actively committed to living my life to follow Jesus since junior high, I've even spent the last 20+ years in ministry as a pastor. Yet, when Renee talks about her relationship with Jesus, there is something inside even me that leaps and longs to taste the intimacy and connection that she clearly has with Him.

In Matthew 18:3, Jesus once said that entering the kingdom of heaven was tied to an ability to change and become like children. There are a lot of ways that Jesus could have finished that sentence after the word change. He could have said, "Unless you change and...

- Become perfect
- Stop making the same mistakes over and over
- Find a church and start attending
- Memorize the bible

You get the idea, right? Jesus could have given us any list of "to-dos" to enter the kingdom of heaven, but what he said was, "unless you change and *become like a child.*" What does that even mean right? Does it mean we have to start pestering Him, "are we there yet"? Does it mean God has to start constantly reminding us to clean our room? Does it mean that we have to start forgetting to feed the dog unless we're reminder every time? Does it, wait, sorry, that was a dad rant! What does it mean though, especially when Jesus attaches this change to something so huge as entering the kingdom of heaven!

I can pretty much guarantee that the people, who heard Jesus say this, were wondering the same thing. Understanding the world Jesus lived in this one sentence from Him had profound cultural implications, social implications, and even religious implications.

Most of all, it had enormous *relational* implications. To a people who had mostly known <u>about</u> God, this was an invitation to know Him, personally, deeply, intimately. This was a people who had only ever known the experience of hearing from God through a prophet or religious leader, a people who related to God in a more formal than relational way. This, invitation to become like a child was about to change everything!

Although my 3 kids are all presently entering the independence of the teen years, we still share a level of closeness and relationship that is unique to what any other human-being experiences with my wife and I because we are mom and dad, and they are our children. Like our children, there is a closeness, a dependence, a trust, a vulnerability, an honesty, even experiences of discipline that all happen in a relationship of love unlike any other.

This is exactly what Jesus is after with us. Like a child!

There is a childlikeness that can be both seen and even felt between Renee and Jesus. What Renee has written here is not theory, it's a reality, her reality, but the amazing thing is, it can be our reality too.

I'm so glad you've picked up this book because you're about to take a journey that I believe will help move you further through a process of change to become more like a child. To know Jesus more deeply, trust Him more fully, love Him more passionately, and to taste what it means that He is our father, our dad. On this journey, you will need to know how to talk to your father and how to hear His voice. What Renee has created here is an incredible tool, born out of her own personal experiences that will help you grow in your ability to chat with Jesus, and experience all the beauty and power that comes from childlike intimacy with Him.

May God bless you on this journey, and may you talk with Him and hear from Him like never before!

—Craig McGlassion

Introduction

This is a thirty-day devotional. What makes this one different from other books or devotionals on prayer? In this devotional, I will introduce you to my dear friend. He is someone who is always there for me. He laughs with me, cries with me, chats with me, and gives me good (and sometimes hard) life lessons. His name is Jesus. Ordinarily, if I wanted you to meet someone, I'd arrange a dinner or coffee date so we could sit down and chat. Unfortunately, I can't invite each of you to either of these things. Instead, I'll tell you about this amazing man who has made such a difference in my life—Jesus, the one I call friend, Savior, and King.

Eventually, I realized He's not just God in heaven, managing the universe and all in it. He's my friend, who enjoys cooking with me, listening to me, and amazing me with His Word and His creation. This is the friend I hope you will discover in this devotional on prayer. I hope you will learn that prayer can become a conversation with Jesus, a chat while you make time for Him.

As you read my memories in this devotional, you may wonder how I interact with Jesus. Do I hear Jesus's voice? What does a conversation look like in real life? My experience and my relationship with Jesus will look different from yours because we are different people. Very seldom does anyone have the same relationship with each person in his or her life; various aspects tailor each relationship, but I hope my story will help you to discover Jesus in your everyday life.

I have been a Christ-follower most of my life, but when I was growing up, Jesus seemed far above me. I knew He loved me and cared about me, but He is the King. Why would He want to be included in my everyday life? If I had a problem, I prayed. I went to church and tried to make reading the Bible a priority.

In my twenties, I realized that He cared about me as a Father and that prayer didn't need to be a formal language addressed to the King. It could be normal conversation, as if I was speaking to another person. I also learned that He wanted to be my go-to person for help in deciphering problems and getting emotional support. I was unloading all my issues on friends and family, but Jesus wanted to be my number-one support. My friends and family could not stand in the place where Jesus was meant to stand. None of those people in my life could meet my needs, nor were they intended to meet the needs that only Jesus could satisfy. This was a huge revelation for me, and so I began a journey of pouring out my heart to Jesus in prayer. It was real and sometimes raw—no emotion held back. This may sound overly dramatic, but this was a challenging season in my life, and Jesus was the best friend to walk me through it. I was learning to trust Him more and to expect less of family and friends. I got what I needed from Him, and anything I received from friends and family was a bonus. This new attitude led to a decreased expectation and more appreciation of those who loved me and cared about me.

As I continued to talk with Jesus about my life and to trust Him with it, I started to see His character and understand who

He was in scripture and while listening to sermons. I began to read the Bible more, but self-application was difficult. In my late twenties, I joined a Bible study group that helped me to understand the Bible and how to apply it to my life. The group used written studies from women who did understand the Bible and the application of it. They knew how to lead their readers to a deeper understanding. This time gave me even more knowledge of Jesus and a greater surrender of my life to Him. It led to trusting Him more and taking risks with Him. I learned to move beyond my fear of failure. I did things He asked of me that seemed impossible and were totally out of my comfort zone. This led to evidence of His power in me. I was being used to help other women in my Bible study group to have a better understanding of scripture, Jesus, and prayer.

In my early thirties, I started getting thoughts of avoiding certain things or going in specific directions. These thoughts usually didn't make sense to me and because the decisions the thoughts affected weren't important, I often dismissed them. After ignoring these thoughts, I discovered that, had I listened, I could have avoided some inconveniences. For example, I had been drinking from a cup while working in the house. When I did laundry, I went to place the now-empty cup on top of the dryer, and the thought popped in my head: *Don't put it there.* There was nothing on the dryer and no apparent reason to avoid this action, so I dismissed the thought and put the cup down. A few minutes later, I knocked the cup with some clothes and just barely caught it before it would have broken on the floor. That was curious to me, I eventually came to the realization that all these seemingly random thoughts were the Holy Spirit. He was trying to help me with my everyday life! That was His inaudible voice popping into my head. This revelation led to prayerful discussions about my conscience. Was my conscience the Holy Spirit? How should I distinguish my own random thoughts from the Holy Spirit?

Recognizing the voice of the Holy Spirit led this adventurer to test that voice. When a thought of guidance or a suggestion that was not sinful or contrary to scripture came to mind, I'd follow it—which direction to take on a journey, to take my car or ride a bike, what to make for dinner and how to I season it, and so on. Sometimes following these suggestions led to help in my life, and other times, I saw no difference. I learned and decided that as long as the direction I thought I was hearing wasn't life-threatening to me or others or contrary to scripture, I would rather follow the suggestion and be wrong than miss something Jesus wanted for me. Recognizing and understanding what was happening in my life and how the Holy Spirit cared about the little details helped me to realize there isn't anything too small for Him to care about.

I often give Jesus credit for the good ideas and choices I have made because of following verses: James 1:17 tells us, "Every good and perfect gift is from above" (KJV). I don't want to take credit for anything because I know that I have to watch pride in my life.

First Corinthians 15:10 reminds me that "but by the grace of God, I am what I am" (NIV), and John 15:5 says, "Apart from Jesus, I can do nothing" (NIV).

I have learned, as I continue to walk with Jesus and make Him a part of my everyday life, that He cares for me, and no detail about my life is too small for Him to notice or to be a part of it.

He loves me that much. And this deep love is not reserved for me; it is available to all. I, like Paul's reference in Ephesians 3:17–19, want you to know how much Jesus loves each of you, more than you can ever imagine or grasp.

Thank you for coming along on the journey with me to discover Jesus in prayer.

"Hello, Friend. I've Been Waiting for You," Says Jesus

Memory

Friend—can I call you *friend*? In my heart, we seem like friends already—this devotional is based on an ongoing chat with Jesus. I will try to bring prayer to you in a different light. During these chats, I have prayed for those who would pick up this book, skim the pages, and take it home. Friend, I'm excited about what you will discover about Jesus as you sit down to chat with Him. It's a different approach, and I'd like to explain how I found it.

When I was a stay-at-home mom, and my kids were in elementary school, I led small groups and participated in women's ministry. This led to more in-depth time reading the Bible, praying, and journaling. I loved it and learned much about Jesus and what a difference a deeper relationship with Him made in my life.

Then I began a full-time job, working the twelve-hour

midnight shift. The kids were in travel soccer and transitioning to middle school and then high school. My life and how I spent my time changed drastically. No more long hours alone with Jesus. I wasn't even reading the Bible every day. I felt guilty about the lack of time I had for Jesus because of the difference in my new schedule. I missed having the time I'd had with Him prior to starting my new job. One morning as I ran out the door, wondering if I'd get time later to quietly read the Bible and pray, I got the impression Jesus was trying to remind me of something. Then I remembered—He isn't about guilt. He's about grace. This new job and the care of my family was where Christ wanted me to be. I was doing what He asked of me. My time looked different, but Jesus wasn't trying to make me feel guilty. He just wanted me to make time for Him. At that moment, a thought popped into my head: *Renee, while you are sitting in the chair, drinking your coffee, trying to wake up, say good morning to Me.*

Wow! I couldn't believe it. Could His grace be that generous? What about the hours I'd spent reading the Bible and praying? There were days for extended time alone with Jesus, but He was helping me to see that, as with other loved ones in my life, I sometimes had a "good morning" with a hug or kiss, and then other times, we would sit down for a meal, have a date, or go on vacation. Jesus wasn't expecting every day to look the same in my time with Him. He just wanted me to acknowledge Him and include Him along the way. How freeing it was for me—no more guilt; now joy and peace.

My friend, take a deep breath. Forget about worrying whether your prayers are perfect or which words to use. Let me introduce you to my friend. Let's have a chat together.

Day 1—Jesus Wants to Call You *Friend*

My summary of John 15:15: Hello, I'm glad you've come today. No matter how much you think you know Me, please believe that I know you. And I don't want to call you *servant*. I want to call you *friend*. A servant doesn't know what his master is doing, but I want you to know all about Me and all I have heard from My Father. Friends share their everyday lives and learn who each other are deep down. What I want for you and Me is a friendship with all the privileges.

Growing up, I learned to pray by listening to our church leaders. Our church language, whether in song or prayers from the pulpit, involved a lot of *thou* and *thee*. We read from the King James version of the Bible, which uses the Old English wording. The prayers I heard when adults prayed and the old hymns we sang sounded regal and formal. God was the Master of the universe, the one who created and ruled everything. I concluded that prayers were to be respectful and proper. I don't remember just talking to God throughout the day until I was in college. I had prayed many prayers, but they were not conversations to a friend; they were proper communication to a King. They lacked intimacy because I did not know intimacy and friendship were part of prayer.

A dear friend had a familiarity with Jesus from the beginning of her relationship with Him. She prayed as if talking with a close friend. There was no *thee* or *thou*; it was a comfortable and familiar conversation.

"Hey, there. I'm having a bad day. I'm not sure what to say, but I know You love me and I know You are listening. It's cool to know You'd listen to someone like me."

Her example changed my whole perspective on prayer. I had read that Jesus wanted to call us *friend*, but I never thought I was worthy to address Him as a friend. Moreover, as a friend, the conversation could be frequent and casual, not only when there was a crisis.

During this exploration of prayer and friendship with Jesus, I read a small book by Brother Lawrence, *The Practice of the Presence of God* (Lawrence 2016). In it, he explains that devotion to God doesn't mean stopping your everyday responsibilities to spend time secluded with Him. It means taking your regular life and including Him in it. As a monk, part of his day included prayer and meditation, but his time with God continued throughout the day. I, too, have learned to incorporate Jesus in my day as Brother Lawrence explained. Over the years, I have learned to chat with Jesus as I would with a loved one. We have talked about my everyday chores and life. When I say "chat," I don't mean that I hear an audible voice or see things, but a thought will pop in my head, or if I'm focused on Him in prayer, I may get a picture of something in my head. I have a pictorial memory, a busy mind, and I think in pictures, just by myself. It's how I remember things. My conversation with Him may look like this:

"What should I make for dinner? Vegetable soup? Perfect for a day like today. Hmm … what spices should I use? Kind of in the mood for cumin. Ooo, chili powder sounds good. Cinnamon? Really? Sounds Indian. Never tried Indian cooking before. Oh, it tastes amazing! Great idea! I love cooking with You."

There are times for more meaningful talks with Him about your concerns or other people in your life, but simple prayers during the day are what I call *chats* with Jesus. We talk things out that are on my mind.

If Jesus wants to call you friend and share all the words the Father has told Him, why wouldn't He want to hear about every aspect of your ordinary life? Isn't that part of the definition of friendship? How will you chat with Jesus right now?

Day 2—Jesus Sees You

My summary of John 1:45–49:
Nathanael sits under an olive tree praying for the Messiah. "God, when will He come, and how will I recognize Him?"
Philip came running up to Nathanael. "I have found the Messiah! Come at once!"
Jesus sees Nathanael coming and says, "Behold, an Israelite indeed, in whom there is no deceit!"
"How do you know me?" asks Nathanael.
"Before Philip called you when you were still under the fig tree, I saw you."
"Rabbi, you are the Son of God! You are the King of Israel!" (Judeo-Christian Research 1999, 2003).

This description of Jesus seeing Nathanael as he prayed under the fig tree is a historical and biblical event, but that doesn't mean that Jesus doesn't do these same things now. "He is the same yesterday, today and forever" (Hebrews 13:8 ESV). Jesus sees each of us, right where we are, no matter where we are in the world. How do we know He sees each of us?

We have evidence throughout the Bible of God creating spaces to be with His people—the garden of Eden, the pillar of fire and cloud in the wilderness, the tabernacle and temple. In Psalms, we read that He knit us together in our mothers' wombs and that He is always there with us and collects our tears. In the Gospels, we read that He knows the number of hairs on our heads. He sees when a sparrow dies. If Jesus is all of these things, doesn't it make sense that He sees you with His eyes? (Genesis 2; Exodus 13:21–22; 40:34; 2 Chronicles 7:1; Psalm 139; 56:8; Matthew 10:29–31; Hebrews 13:5). Can you believe these things for yourself? It's a concept that is not always easy to grasp or believe.

In Mark 9:14–24, a father comes to Jesus for the healing of his son, but he has trouble believing that Jesus can do this miracle. He cries out to Jesus to help his unbelief. This blows my mind! Jesus asks us to believe, but He also helps us to do that very thing. We don't have to believe in our own strength. In John 20:26–29, we read of Thomas's doubting the other disciples' account of Jesus's resurrection. Jesus does not shun Thomas. Instead, He takes the time to answer Thomas's questions and bring peace. Jesus does not reject us in our difficulty to believe Him and His Word. He wants us to ask Him for help in our unbelief and doubt.

Jesus sees you and loves you right now. It is my hope and prayer, as you continue with this devotional, that you will find Jesus and the answers to some of your questions. Are you having trouble believing that Jesus sees you? Have you asked Him to help your unbelief?

Day 3—Jesus Waits for You

> *Now he had to go through Samaria. So he came to a town in Samaria called Sychar, near the plot of ground Jacob had given to this son Joseph. Jacob's*

well was there, and Jesus, tired as he was from the journey, sat down by the well. It was about noon.
(John 4:4–6 NIV)

These verses on their own seem bland and might be overlooked. A man sits at a well at noon after a long journey. Don't you think that a walk at noon on what was most likely a hot day was odd? Another thing to consider is that Jewish people were not allowed to associate with the Samaritan people. This expectation was due to much historical hostility between the Samaritans and the Jews. Also, the Samaritans were considered unclean, due in part to their having intermarried with the Assyrians hundreds of years earlier. Some commentaries and historians go so far as to say that, biologically, they weren't even Jews, but they assumed a form of Jewish practices (Bible Study Tools 2019, 17.2.2).

Jesus takes the time to journey—at noon in the hot sun—through Samaria to sit and wait at a well. He is waiting for this woman— this woman, specifically. He is waiting to share the gospel message with her. We learn later in the chapter that this woman has had five husbands but is now living with a man who is not her husband. Some commentators (Christian Stack Exchange 2013) have concluded that her community had shunned her, leading her to draw water at noon, when most drew water in the morning and the evening. She was avoiding her neighbors—their comments and looks. Again, however, Jesus does not reject her. He waits specifically for her, not avoiding her. Jesus receives her as a woman, a Samaritan, and a sinner. He declares that He is the Messiah for whom she is waiting to explain everything to her— eternal life through Him.

Why would Jesus come to this woman? In reading the gospel account of Jesus, we learn that one of His missions on earth was to model to all of us how to live a life that brings honor and glory to the Father. His life was spent demonstrating this to all. In the last days before Jesus ascended to heaven, He told the disciples to take the gospel to the whole world (Matthew 28:18–20). Second Peter 3:9 tells us the Lord is patient, not wishing any to perish. This account is one example of the lengths to which Jesus is willing to go to bring a message of hope, forgiveness, and life to someone.

Please know that you too are worth Jesus's time. Jesus is quietly waiting for you, wherever you may be at this moment. Whether others consider you as acceptable or unacceptable, Jesus has already come to meet you and is waiting for you to acknowledge His presence and chat with Him. He wants to share His life with you. Will you share your day with Him?

Day 4—Listening to Jesus

> As Jesus and his disciples were on their way, he came to a village where a woman named Martha opened her home to him. She had a sister called Mary, who sat at the Lord's feet listening to what he said. But Martha was distracted by all the preparations needing to be made. She came to him and asked, "Lord, don't you care that my sister has left me to do the work by myself? Tell her to help me!" "Martha, Martha," the Lord answered, "you are worried and upset about many things, but few things are needed—or indeed only one. Mary has

chosen what is better, and it will not be taken away
from her." (Luke 10:38–42 NIV)

Jesus pops over for dinner! What would you do—have a conversation, listen, or prepare the food?

Let's focus on Mary's response. She chooses to sit at Jesus's feet while her sister makes the meal. Jesus does not rebuke Martha's choice to make dinner but references her being "worried and upset about many things." Mary is close to Him and focused on what He is saying. Martha is close enough to see Mary seated at His feet. Martha could have quietly prepared dinner while listening to Him, but she chooses to be worried and upset.

We have learned that Jesus wants to be our friend. He sees each of us right where we are and is waiting patiently for each of us. What response does He require?

When we consider the message of the entire scripture, we learn that Jesus has come to give each of us a message of love, a deeper understanding of who He is, and why we are important to Him. Sometimes we may think the only reason to believe and accept His gift of salvation is to avoid hell. It's true that He came to die on the cross so we might be in heaven, but He also wants to be in our lives right now. He wants to be our friend and share in our lives now. He died to be in a relationship with us.

How do you listen to Jesus and have a relationship with Him? When do you do this? How much time do you need for this? We each have our own times of day that we set aside for Jesus— different schedules or mind-sets. I am very easily distracted and require more time to accommodate the distractions. On my way to work, however, I'm very focused on my conversation with Jesus.

If there is a response from Him, my mind is clear enough to catch it quickly. He knows me and knows how to communicate with me. I understand and love Him and don't want to miss Him; therefore, I have disciplined myself to wake up early to be available.

For an action to become a habit, we must do that action for two weeks. Maybe this is the time to begin a pattern of sitting at the feet of Jesus and listening to Him. Look at yourself and your schedule to determine when you are best able to listen and focus. Then try it for two weeks to create a new habit of listening to Jesus.

Day 5—Can You Hear Him?

> *In the beginning was the Word, and the Word was with God, and the Word was God. And the Word became flesh and dwelt among us, and we have seen his glory, glory as of the only son from the Father, full of grace and truth. (John 1:1, 14 ESV)*

Have friends or family members ever told you about their exciting vacation or a great movie they watched? You may listen, and sometimes you may be excited for them, but you cannot completely understand what they're talking about because you haven't experienced it for yourself. It's the same way with understanding who Jesus is. We can listen to preachers, teachers, friends, or family members talk about Jesus and the Bible, but until we spend time in prayer and reading the Bible, we cannot know for ourselves what it means to understand Him and get to know Him.

When you read the Bible, you will discover the person of

Jesus and eventually get some idea of how He would answer the questions you have for Him. Paul tells us, "There's nothing like the written Word of God for showing you the way to salvation through faith in Christ Jesus. Every part of Scripture is God-breathed and useful one way or another—showing us the truth, exposing our rebellion, correcting our mistakes, training us to live God's way" (2 Timothy 3:15–16 MSG).

Every part of scripture is from God through the instruction of the Holy Spirit, who helps us to understand what we are reading and to learn who Jesus is and what a relationship with Him looks like for each of us. Friends, we may not see Jesus face-to-face, as we'd like, but He has not left us alone. We have His Word written down for us and His Spirit to interact with us.

> *But the Counselor, the Holy Spirit—the Father will send Him in My name—will teach you all things and remind you of everything I have told you. (John 14:26 HCSB)*

We can learn and understand the scripture and become familiar with the person of Jesus by reading His Word and believing that His Spirit will help us to understand what we are reading and to find the answers we are looking for in this life. Caution, however, is needed here. When reading scripture, don't make the mistake of taking a verse out of a certain chapter or book and say, "This is it! I have my answer!" Look at the whole chapter and to whom the author is speaking and what subject the author is discussing. If you are unclear about the meaning of scripture, go to a friend more familiar with the Bible, a small-group leader, or your pastor. Read commentaries and other Bible study tools.

Proverbs 19:20 reminds us that it is *wise* to seek advice and accept instruction.

Remember that Jesus not only wants to listen to you, but He also enjoys responding to you. He loves you deeply. Read His Word to discover Him and recognize His voice in your life. Ask Him now for help in identifying His voice.

Wrap-Up

We have learned that Jesus sees us and has come for each of us. He waits for us. He listens to our prayers. Our part is to respond to His pursuit, read the Bible, and look for Him. We should talk to Jesus as a friend or family member, not as a King, too high above us to hear our prayers. We learned from Nathanael to pray expectantly. We learned from the Samaritan woman to listen to Jesus and believe that He does not come to condemn but to offer everlasting life. From Mary, we saw quiet and undistracted listening. Finally, we touched on how to hear from Jesus and discern His voice and His answers to our prayers.

The message of the entire Bible tells us God has always wanted to be in a relationship with every one of us. He makes a place for us to do life with Him. When we reject Him in sin, Jesus comes and makes a way. Every time we refuse His way, God returns with love, mercy, grace, and forgiveness, trying to be in our lives. Christ paid the ultimate price for our sin and made it possible to be in an unhampered, personal relationship with God, the Father. When we realize this message and believe it, we are adopted into the family of God, sons and daughters of the Most High God. We become friends of Jesus when we make it a point to live a life of obedience to Him.

The idea of friendship with Jesus is an enormous thought; it may take a while to wrap your head around it, but bit by bit, the concept and understanding of it will sink in and become exceedingly, abundantly more than you can ever imagine (Ephesians 3:20).

Just take a moment, right where you are, and spend some time with my friend, Jesus. Share a thought or a "Wow!" or a thank-you for what you've learned in this week's readings. He'd love to chat about it.

TWO

The Unusual Suspects

Memory

Just a little background about why I too am an unusual suspect for Jesus's work to help others—or at least I thought I was. I refer to myself, in part, as a recovering people-pleaser. Part of my makeup is to be a rule follower and to submit to those in authority over me. Some would say these are characteristics of the firstborn, but it's just how I'm wired. That doesn't mean I don't fight against authority or break the rules at times, but overall, my mind-set is to follow the rules.

Put that mind-set together with a feeling that I don't belong or don't fit in or I'm not good enough. For no known reason, I have felt this inadequacy since I was about five years old. Those two things—the rule-follower mind-set and my feeling inadequate—created a people-pleaser. I believed that if I performed in a certain way, I could gain someone's love and acceptance. Even if I thought I already had that love and acceptance, I still wanted to please the person to keep it. The desire to please ran deep in my heart, deeper than I ever imagined. I was brought up with a strict moral and religious code, which led me to believe that although my salvation was free and required no work, Jesus would love me less if I disobeyed.

Recovering from people-pleasing tendencies took years of Bible study and chatting with Jesus. Then one day, Jesus revealed my heart's secret motivation—the final piece I needed to guard my heart against the sin of people-pleasing. It blew my mind and sent me into brief despair that I had not known until that day.

My other compulsion that I was working on with Jesus was my controlling nature. To be a successful people-pleaser, you need to control your environment and people's response to you. These two things—control and people-pleasing—were a part of me that went deeper than I realized. That final piece Jesus revealed was that many times, my good intentions and acts of kindness were used to gain someone's love and approval. I manipulated people into caring for me. I have a way of making people feel loved. People appreciate that in me. It's a good thing, designed by Jesus to show His love toward others through me, but my deceitful heart twisted it into manipulation.

I was horrified and overwhelmed with gratitude at the same time. I would have tossed someone like me right out the door if I'd known that. But not Jesus! He not only kept me, but He managed to use that gift to bless others and change my old motivation. Who loves like that? Who forgives and extends mercy like that? Jesus does.

Over the next few days, we will look at the surprising love of Jesus and those He chooses to have on His team and to associate with while on earth. His love, mercy, and forgiveness are greater than we can ever imagine.

Day 1—The Thief

My summary of Matthew 9:9–13:

Jesus saw a man named Matthew sitting at the tax collector's booth. "Follow me," He told him, and Matthew followed Him. Jesus had dinner at Matthew's house with many tax collectors and sinners. The Pharisees saw this and asked, "Why does your teacher eat with tax collectors and sinners?" Jesus heard this and answered, "I have not come to call the righteous, but the sinners."

My summary of Luke 19:1–10:

Jesus was passing through Jericho, and Zacchaeus, a short man who was a tax collector, climbed a tree to see Jesus above the crowd. Jesus came up to the tree and called him down from the tree and invited Himself to stay at Zacchaeus's house. As people again questioned Jesus's choice of company, Zacchaeus repented of his greed and declared he would give to the poor and pay back those he had cheated, four times the amount. Jesus once again declared, "The Son of Man came to seek and to save the lost."

How many tax collectors do you know? Even though they are not known for being swindlers, many people do not have a high opinion of that vocation. A friend of mine accepted a job at the IRS (America's tax agency) and felt he had to justify his choice and defend his character. He is an honorable man, yet he faced unwarranted bias of the job Jesus led him to accept.

In Jesus's time, society despised tax collectors for many reasons, but one reason was that they worked for the ruling foreign government, Rome. Rome historically was barbaric and greedy with regard to the countries and people they ruled. Tax collectors were Jews who worked for the enemy and took money from family and neighbors. One way the tax collectors got their money was to overcharge. A person would not want to be associated with these social outcasts and risk becoming an outcast along with them, and I imagine no one would want to be invited to a tax collector's home. Jesus, however, doesn't live by the laws of society. He lives by the law of grace, mercy, and love.

Did you catch the immediate response of Matthew and Zacchaeus? Matthew leaves his lucrative job to follow a rabbi—in this context, a rabbi without a home—where there is no mention of income. Zacchaeus has Jesus as a guest in his home. He immediately confesses his sin and declares how he will make amends for those sins. These two outcasts of society immediately respond to Jesus's attention and lack of judgment. He doesn't come to them with a list of their faults. He asks each of these men to follow Him—Matthew to follow into ministry and Zacchaeus to his home. Jesus demonstrates attention and love. Jesus doesn't point out the sin until the watchers begin questioning. Did you see Jesus's word choice? He doesn't point His finger at Matthew or Zacchaeus. He says to all who can hear that He has come to call the sinners; to seek and save the lost. He wasn't just speaking to the "obvious" sinners in the crowd but to all who had ears to hear. Paul tells us in Romans 3:23, "All have sinned and fall short of the glory of God" (NIV).

Jesus went right to the outcasts. By singling them out and

being with each of them, He invited them into a dignity they didn't think was attainable. Have you, like these men, ever felt like an outcast, as if you don't quite measure up to the standards of those near you? Jesus will come to you, offering unbiased love.

Day 2—The Adulteress

My summary of John 8:2–11:

At dawn, Jesus appeared again in the temple courts, where all the people gathered around Him, and He sat down to teach them. The teachers of the Law and the Pharisees brought in a woman caught in the act of adultery. They made her stand before the group and asked Jesus, "Teacher, this woman is an adulterer, and in the Law of Moses, such a woman should be stoned. What do you say?" This was a trap for Jesus, and He said nothing. He bent down, wrote in the dirt, and said, "Let any of you who is without sin throw the first stone." He bent down again and resumed His writing. As he wrote, one by one her accusers left until none remained. After some time, Jesus asked, "Woman, where are they? Has no one condemned you?" She replied, "No one, sir." Jesus declared, "Then neither do I condemn you. Go now, and leave your life of sin."

For God did not send His Son into the world to condemn the world, but to save the world through Him. (John 3:17 NIV)

Can we start with when this occurs? Jesus has come to the temple, where people are waiting to hear Him teach, and in comes the religious rulers. They have brought a woman caught in the act of adultery at dawn. How did they find this woman in the morning and not at night, as the couple began their evening? Where was the man? How did they know she'd been having an affair, and why did they bring her out now? These were a few questions I had while writing this.

Often in scripture, Jesus doesn't respond to the question posed to Him but asks a question of His own. The teachers of the Law and the Pharisees who attempted to trap Him into breaking the Law ended up being the victims of their own trap. Jesus offered no spoken words, accusing no one. However, one by one, they left until only the accused woman and Jesus remained in front of the crowd gathered for teaching.

Jesus told her He did not condemn her, but notice how he finished: "Go now, and leave your life of sin." Jesus acknowledged her actions as sin and instructed her to leave the sin, but He did not condemn her.

Jesus knows that we are all sinners, but He has not come to pass judgment for that sin or give us our just punishment for sin.

The people came to hear a lesson from Jesus, and their first lesson was an example of His forgiveness, mercy, and love.

What of the woman in this scene? She was used to trap Jesus and distract the people from hearing a message from Him. When people rooted in law vehemently accuse you of sin, don't allow their words and actions to distract you from Jesus's message of forgiveness, mercy, and love. He has not come to condemn you but to save you from the power and penalty of sin. Remember the people in the Bible at whom we have looked thus far. None of these people is perfect. Some of them are more socially accepted, but none is perfect. We have to learn to tune out the messages of the crowd that say we don't measure up and turn off those same messages replaying in our minds. We must read the Bible and listen to words from the Bible and songs that point us to Jesus so we can replace those lies with His truth.

He took this woman, drowning in shame, and lifted her head to see Him and the love He offered—a love without shame—and the ability to free her from sin and shame.

Just as in this depiction of the adulterous woman, Jesus will ask you to leave your sin at some point. He has not come into the world to shame us, but He has to point out our sin so that we may ask for forgiveness and depart from that sin. The confession of our sin and making steps to turn from it will lead us to a more intimate relationship with Him.

Is there shame distracting you from seeing and hearing Jesus's message of love and forgiveness? Is there a sin that Jesus has mentioned that you are having trouble eliminating from your life? The love of Jesus covers every sin and frees us from the power of sin. You are not alone. He is with you.

For more details about understanding this power over sin and the freedom Jesus offers, visit www.wecanbefree.org (Stanley 2012) for a free message from Andy Stanley, the senior pastor of North Point Community Church, in Alpharetta, Georgia.

Day 3—The Deceiver

> *God said to Moses, "Say to the Israelites, 'The LORD, the God of your fathers—the God of Abraham, the God of Isaac and the God of Jacob—has sent me to you.'" (Exodus 3:15 NIV)*

After this, his brother came out, with his hand grasping Esau's heel; so he was named Jacob. (Genesis 25:26 NIV)

Who is this Jacob of the Old Testament, the man honorably mentioned with the name of God, used to remind the Israelites of God's covenant made with them and the special place they hold with God? (Got Questions 2019) His is a story that takes nearly half of the book of Genesis to tell. In short, Jacob failed to follow God consistently or love his family well. God chose Jacob and included him in the name He calls Himself.

From the beginning of his story, Jacob is described as making war with his brother, in and out of the womb. He was named for being a supplanter (Behind the Name 2019), a deceiver, and someone who was treacherous (Merriam-Webster June). Jacob stole his brother Esau's birthright and blessing, due to his being the firstborn son. He did this by deceiving his old and nearly blind father. Then Jacob ran for his life to his uncle's land. During his stay with his uncle, he became a victim of his father-in-law's deceit and played favorites with his children, just as his parents did to him and Esau. He had two wives, two lovers, and thirteen children—and much-accumulated wealth.

When you read the story of Jacob, you discover this man is not a rule follower. He is cunning and even deceitful in gaining wealth and advantage. John Darby, a nineteenth-century English Bible teacher, describes in his commentary Jacob's relationship with God as "God dealing with a soul that does not walk with Him. It is not, however, the consistent communion of Abraham with Jehovah. God is seen dealing with him, and Jacob, in a measure, is seen thinking on God; but proper communion is not there" (Darby 1970).

Jacob may seem like an odd person to add to this chapter, but his life highlights the love and faithfulness of God and His pursuit of everyone, even the deceiver. Many of us deceive ourselves into thinking that we can earn our relationship with Jesus. We may think if we mold ourselves to a certain standard, He will recognize us and have a relationship with us. There are benefits to obedience to Jesus, as laid out in the New Testament (e.g., John 15). However, do not think that Jesus won't have a relationship with you until you fix this or that. That is not an accurate perception of His love and faithfulness to us. His love is about grace, mercy, and forgiveness.

When you come to Jesus in prayer, seeking a conversation, He, in His mercy, doesn't look at your sin or character flaws. He sees the one He created, the one for whom He died on the cross, the one He has been waiting to talk to alone. If God will remain faithful to His covenant promise through a man like Jacob, why wouldn't Jesus remain faithful to His new covenant and offer you a relationship with Him?

Day 4—The Escape Artist

In the Old Testament books of Exodus, Leviticus, Numbers, and Deuteronomy, we find the testimony of Moses's life, written by him, with God's inspirational assistance. It is a saga of one man chosen by God to lead God's people from their slavery in Egypt and bring them to the land promised to their forefathers— Abraham, Isaac, and Jacob.

We read about Moses being rescued by Pharaoh's daughter from the royal decree to kill all Hebrew male babies. He was brought up in the royal household with all the privileges and training that came with it. At age forty, Moses witnessed the beating of a Hebrew slave, and he killed the Egyptian guard responsible. He fled to Midian to escape execution. There, he met a woman named Zipporah and began a new life. After forty years in Midian, God called out to Moses from a burning bush (that was not consumed by the fire). He talked out loud to Moses, the escape artist hiding in the desert. Moses then argued with God about His request to have Moses lead the Israelites out of Egypt. Moses was frightened and didn't take into account the incredible privilege of having this encounter with God. After some concession from God, Moses began his journey by disobeying God and not circumcising his son and was nearly killed by God. Zipporah rescued him by performing the circumcision herself.

This was the beginning of Moses's life of service with God. Despite this man's shaky start with God and his criminal past, God chose Moses to represent Him. Moses followed and obeyed God along his journey to lead the Israelites out of Egypt and to the Promised Land. He spent so much time with "the Lord talking face to face as a man speaking to a friend" (Exodus 33:11 ESV) that his face shone with radiance (Exodus 34:29–35). It frightened the Israelites. So he kept his face veiled until he went into the tent to meet with God. Moses's task from God was very hard, but he was never without God.

> The Lord said to Moses, "I will do the very thing
> you have asked (His Presence with the Israelites)
> because I am pleased with you." (Exodus 33:17 NIV)

Don't ever think there is so much badness in you that you can't be a friend of God or be used by Him. God reached out to Moses before one act of obedience or having a relationship. Moses's life that followed was a result of God's invitation, and Moses continued to respond in obedience and repentance.

In the *Asbury Bible Commentary*, authors Eugene E. Carpenter and Wayne McCown note that "obedience does not produce a relationship with God, it is in response to and maintenance of an already existing relationship." Through this devotional, you are reading about Jesus's pursuit of you in a relationship. When you respond with your own pursuit of Him, you will desire to be obedient to Him and align yourself with His ways, as laid out in the Bible.

Are you hiding from something, like Moses? Are you hiding from Jesus? He has found you. I hope you are discovering Him in the pages of this devotional. How will you respond? How will you attempt to pursue Him? You are already doing so by reading this devotional. Are you finding it easier to chat with Him?

Day 5—The Executioner

Then they cast him [Stephen] out of the city and stoned him. And the witnesses laid down their garments at the feet of the young man named Saul.
(Acts 7:58 ESV)

These verses are the first mention of Paul in the gospel. Here, he is known as Saul. He was a Zealot. "The Zealots were Pharisees who advocated violent resistance against anyone who would claim to be a Ruler or Lord who was not Israel's God" (LaPort 2013). The Pharisees were a distinguished Jewish sect that strictly followed the rules of the Torah and were known for creating many of their own rules to "assist" the people in honoring God. They were known for their pretentious piety and elitism. Saul was a Roman citizen, and Rome was the barbaric ruling authority in Israel.

Let's review: a Jewish Roman citizen, a Pharisee, a Zealot, and one in charge of hunting down Christians for imprisonment and possibly death (Got Questions 2019). Would Paul be your first choice to become a missionary? Put yourself in the shoes of a Jewish Christ follower. Would you think that this man needed Jesus and so you would talk to him? I don't know.

As you read through the entire Bible, you will notice that God does not do much of anything as we would do. Jesus, instead, catches up with Saul on the way to persecute the Christians in Damascus. Jesus gives Saul a face-to-face meeting. A bright light from heaven suddenly overtakes Saul, causing him to fall to the ground, and Jesus asks him, "Why are you persecuting Me?" Saul asks, "Who are you, Lord?" He replies, "I am Jesus" (Acts 9:1–5).

It is the beginning of the Saul's mission, also known as Paul, author of thirteen books of the New Testament and missionary to nearly fifty cities. To completely understand the scope of this man's contribution to Christianity, begin by reading the New Testament letters. The first letter found in the New Testament is Romans.

Jesus knew Paul's heart, one devoted to the Law and the ways of the Jewish faith. He just needed to redirect Paul. Did you notice how quickly Paul did his about-face? He was a man known to be a Zealot. He was not a weak-minded man. After just one encounter with Jesus, however, this unusual suspect humbled himself to go where Jesus told him to go. He learned who Jesus was and committed his life to obey Him.

How about you? Do you, like Saul, consider yourself to have done horrible things? Have you, like Saul, had an encounter with Jesus? Was your response like Saul's, laying down pride and, in humility, embracing obedience? When faced with a decision to follow Jesus, remember that He sees your heart and what you can become with Him in your life.

Wrap-Up

What incredible stories we read this week. The love of Jesus is immense and indescribable. He has a way of looking beyond the obvious and the stereotypes. Jesus sees right to the heart and knows what will become of the person whose heart responds to Him. Did you notice the various responses to God from each of these people? Jesus took the time to interact with each one. Jesus came to them to display His character, not to put a spotlight on theirs. Jesus offered them love, forgiveness, and an opportunity to be freed from sin and the shame of sin and to respond to that forgiveness and love. You can't be too far away, as in the case of Moses, hiding in the desert; too lofty and influential, as was Saul; too far gone, as with Matthew, Zacchaeus, and the adulteress; or too self-serving, as was Jacob.

Jesus can see the life you can have with Him—the abundant life, free from sin, shame, and the power of sin. Jesus says often in scripture that He came to save the lost, heal the sick, and rescue the imprisoned. He came to love, forgive, and set each of us free.

Never underestimate the difference Jesus can make in your life and how He can influence many more through a life lived in obedience to Jesus.

Who are you? Where do you find yourself right now? Can you still say that you don't measure up? Remember it's not about what you bring to Jesus. It's about your answering Him and saying yes. Everything else is up to Him. We follow the one who calls us, loves us, and wants to do amazing things in and through every one of us.

❧ Three ❧

Bow or Curtsy?
How Do I Approach the King?

Memory

Have you ever read the Bible from cover to cover? Did you feel satisfaction in knowing that you had read every word of it? Or was there sorrow because it had come to an end, because the world you had walked into while reading was done? Maybe you missed some of the characters. If you don't enjoy reading, you may not understand that sentiment.

It was many years before I made the time to read the Bible all the way through, which took over a year. I didn't feel sorrow when I finished reading but excitement. I had read every word, and I could see patterns and discover more of God and His character in those pages.

In the Bible, I read about many different conversations with God. Some were words of pleading and sorrow. Others were words of praise, discussion, or questions for direction while being obedient to God's requests. After reading about the many people mentioned in the Bible, I discovered there is no one way to pray to our Lord. He created us so He could be in a relationship with us. Can a person instruct you on how to talk to a friend? There may be suggestions, but it has been my experience that as I get to know a person, I learn how to communicate with that person individually. It is the same with Jesus. He asks that you hear Him and listen to His words. He desires that you respond to Him and include Him in your everyday life.

Moreover, just as Jesus helps us with our unbelief, He will help us figure out how the conversation will look with Him. There are times when I laugh out loud about something, other times when I concentrate on a question or problem, and other times when I'm half asleep, trying to wake up and say good morning. As with any person, you can see with your eyes and hear with your ears, and a rhythm will develop that is unique to you and Jesus. It may be awkward at first, but keep pursuing Him and responding to Him.

If you wander around in the many psalms in the Bible, you will find where David is distraught, seeks vengeance, and lays out to God precisely what he wants done. I was surprised at how raw and angry he is when he speaks to God. David actually tells God the methods he hopes God will use to avenge him. That is bold and honest. It helped me to come to God in any circumstance, with any emotion I found myself at the time. He can handle my grief, my anger, and my confusion. His love is so big that, like David, no feeling you have will keep Him from hearing your prayers and listening.

Day 1—Postures of the Heart

You will seek me and find me when you seek me
with all your heart. (Jeremiah 29:13 ESV)

I appreciate the following quote from the Institute in Basic Life Principles: "Communication with God does not require a certain physical position, but postures do give expression to the attitudes of our hearts."

As you become familiar with the Bible and read through the history of biblical characters, you will learn of many different ways to pray and physical postures of prayer. No physical posture or specific words carry more weight than others. As stated in Jeremiah 29:13, it is an attitude of the heart. Jesus is interested and waiting to hear from each of us in our times of need, rejoicing, doubt, fear, excitement, and exploring.

The posture and the words depend on the reason for your chat with Jesus and the attitude of your heart. Sometimes I have come to Jesus angry, and there has been yelling and crying. Other times, I have been silent and lay flat on the floor, listening. There also has been everything in between. My posture depends on my need at the time and the surroundings in which I find myself during that chat.

Just as in face-to-face conversations with people, there are different volumes to your words, different body positions, and various gestures or positions of your arms and hands. Some words are whispered out of respect or confidentiality. Others are loud with excitement, frustration, delight, or even anger or determination. Gestures can include merely talking with your hands, reaching out and gently touching someone as you speak, crossing your arms, folding your hands in anticipation—the list is endless. So it is with prayer. Your posture will depend on the location—sitting or lying down or standing. You can intentionally kneel in humility, displaying submission to Jesus; bow in honor before your King; or lift your arms in admiration and praise or even in desperation because you need Him at that moment.

As with postures, there are many different attitudes of prayer that can be explored, both in the Bible and on your favorite search engine. While praying about this day's devotion and searching online, I came to this attitude mentioned in Jeremiah 29:13. In this verse is the assurance that no matter what your emotion, intention, or mood at the time of seeking Jesus in prayer, if you seek Him with your whole heart, you will find Him. The point is concise and straightforward, filled with much-needed confidence. We have something to say, and we want someone to listen to us. Jesus will listen.

The short answer to which posture we should assume in prayer is to come to Jesus; He is a friend who is willing to listen with all of His heart and attention. Take a moment to express whatever emotion you are feeling. Talk silently in your head, or out loud while alone—whatever. Speak, and He will listen.

Day 2—Walking with Jesus

> *When Enoch had lived 65 years, he fathered Methuselah. Enoch walked with God after he fathered Methuselah 300 years and had other sons and daughters. Thus, all the days of Enoch were 365 years. Enoch walked with God. (Genesis 5:21–25 ESV)*

*But I say, walk by the Spirit, and you will not gratify
the desires of the flesh. (Galatians 5:16 ESV)*

Walking with Jesus—what does that look like or mean? Two or more people agree to move in one direction together. They are side by side or in a group, usually with one person leading the way or two in cooperation with each other. There is communication of one sort or another—at the very least, there's discussion about the direction and destination—and then possibly silence along the way. I would imagine each pair's or group's conversation would look different, depending on the agreed-upon purpose.

When paralleling prayer with walking alongside Jesus, I would suggest that one way of praying is basically walking through life *with* Jesus. John 15:5 reminds us that apart from Jesus, we accomplish nothing. In walking through life with Jesus, whether in conversation or silence, there is communion with our movement. There is the possibility of an understanding of which direction your path should take and which potholes to avoid along the way. Psalm 119:105 says that the Bible is a lamp unto our feet. John 1:1 and 1:14 tells us that Jesus is the Word made flesh. The continuity of scripture paints an understanding that the lamp unto our feet is Jesus, and He will guide our steps. When we walk with Him in communion and with faith, we can experience the full, abundant life He offers (John 10:10).

I hope you will look the scripture passages I've mentioned. Reading scripture shows us how to walk with Christ, whether in silence or conversation. We will soon recognize His voice and character. When we say that we want to walk alongside Jesus as an expression of our prayer, we cannot forget that He is indeed the scriptures, and these words help us to come alongside Him in our everyday lives. These are His words, inspired by His Spirit, describing His personality. We soon will move when He moves, stop when He stops, see the potholes ahead, and become "surefooted as a deer; enabling us to stand on mountain heights" (Psalm 18:33 NLT).

Unfortunately, we cannot physically see Jesus and watch His pace or the literal direction He takes at any given moment. The more we chat with Him, however, and read the scriptures, the more mindful we are of His presence in our lives. And the more we are mindful, the more frequently, when a thought pops into our heads, we can refer to the scriptural knowledge of Jesus's character and determine that the idea is from Him.

Are you taking regular walks with Jesus?

Day 3—Regular Prayer

> He [Daniel] went to his house where he had windows in his upper chamber open toward Jerusalem. He got down on his knees three times a day and prayed and gave thanks before his God, as he had done previously. (Daniel 6:10 ESV)

> But Jesus often withdrew to lonely places and prayed. (Luke 5:16 NIV)

In the above verses, we see that Daniel, an Israelite, was taken from his home and into captivity in Babylon. He quickly found favor with the ruler, who later gave him much responsibility in

Babylon. He prayed alone in his house three times a day, without shame, at an open window that faced Jerusalem. And Jesus withdrew to lonely places, undistracted, and prayed.

Daniel and Jesus made prayer a regular part of their everyday lives. They prayed without shame, so others were aware of it, but in seclusion, so they were alone with the Father and had limited distractions. Prayer was a dedicated time to be with God in conversation. When you read the book of Daniel and the first four books of the New Testament—Matthew, Mark, Luke, and John—you will discover no record of the words prayed by either of these men. They were each alone with God, and the discussion was private. What we do read is that they prayed regularly. These men were both known to withdraw alone to pray to God. Both were respected by those with whom they interacted on an everyday basis. They were known for their wisdom and extraordinary abilities while obeying God right where they were. Each of them dared to obey God and not man. Each man held to the authority of man but found victory in the faithfulness of God. Those times alone gave each of them the strength and ability to be effective in the place God had them.

I am so glad there are no recorded lines of their words. There is nothing for us to compare our prayers to in this instance. The point is that each of us is to have regular, solitary time in prayer. Do you spend time in prayer so often that you'd miss it if it didn't happen? Can you be described as a woman/man of prayer? Don't feel guilty if your answer is no. It's just a heart check to talk with Jesus in your conversations with Him.

Take a moment to ponder where you are in your relationship with Jesus—casual acquaintances, buddies, or best friends? Where would you like to be with Jesus?

Day 4—Just Be Real, and Don't Hold Back

He withdrew about a stone's throw beyond them, knelt and prayed, 'Father, if you are willing, take this cup from me; yet not my will, but yours be done.' An angel from heaven appeared to him and strengthened him. And being in anguish, he prayed more earnestly, and his sweat was like drops of blood falling to the ground. (Luke 22:41–44 NIV)

You deceived me, Lord, and I was deceived; you overpowered me and prevailed. I am ridiculed all day long; everyone mocks me. Whenever I speak, I cry out proclaiming violence and destruction. The word of the Lord has brought me insult and reproach all day long … but the LORD is with me like a mighty warrior; so my persecutors will stumble and not prevail. (Jeremiah 20:7–8 NIV)

Break the teeth in their mouths, O God; Lord, tear out the fangs of those lions! Let them vanish like water that flows away; when they draw the bow, let their arrows fall short. May they be like a slug that melts away as it moves along, like a stillborn child that never sees the sun. Before your pots can feel the heat of the thorns—whether they be green or dry— the wicked will be swept away. (Psalm 58:6–9 NIV)

These snapshots of various prayers and cries to the Most High God reveal to us that these people held nothing back—anguish, sorrow, fear, and vengeance all laid out before the Lord. There was freedom in the relationship with God.

God is all-knowing; why not just verbalize what's inside? Nothing is hidden from Him. He is big enough to hear our deepest feelings shouted out and cried out to Him. We read in the passage above from Luke that Jesus was in so much anguish that He sweat drops of blood. He knew that He could bare His heart to His Father, and the Father would listen, offer support, and be present with Him.

In the passage above, Jeremiah is following the Lord's instructions, and the people are not listening. Destruction and punishment come upon his family, neighbors, and city. He watches all of it and begins to mourn. He also is mocked, beaten, and imprisoned for his obedience to the Lord. He cries out to God and holds nothing back. His submission to God is painful, and it is made worse by the treatment he suffers and the people's unwillingness to obey God and turn back to Him. Jeremiah lets God know exactly how he feels. Nothing is held back.

Finished with the pursuit and betrayal of "friends," David brought it to God and held nothing back. His prayers (also known as the psalms) were songs to God—laid out to music, even. He wanted vengeance and was very specific about how God should carry it out, and he expressed it in the way he was comfortable talking with God—through song and music. Again, God knew his heart and heard it all.

Bringing it all to Jesus in an honest and real way is not the end of the conversation. Remember we are learning how to have a conversation with Jesus. The discussion involves two people talking and listening to each other. Let's see how each of these men handled their intense prayers. We read in Luke 22:43 that an angel appeared to Jesus in the garden and offered Him strength. Then Jesus stood up and walked into the hands of the guards who sought Him.

Jeremiah let it all out and then, in later verses, proclaimed the might of the Lord, singing and praising Him for who He is, despite Jeremiah's dismal condition. David may have asked God to avenge him, but he never took it upon himself to exact that revenge. He submitted to the Lord and endured his trials while waiting on the perfect timing of the Lord. You can find evidence of this in 1 Samuel 24. Each of these men knew it was safe to bare their souls, but they also recognized the authority of the one to whom they prayed and submitted in obedience and praise.

Where does that leave us? How is this applicable to our prayers and conversations with Jesus? Our God is big. His love is deep and wide. He wants to hear our every word. Hebrews 13:8 tells us that Jesus is the same yesterday, today, and tomorrow. We are learning of His great love for each of us. He loved and listened to men in the Bible. He will listen to you. He hasn't changed. He offers His ear to help us bare our souls and release any emotion we have at that moment. However, once the feelings are out for that moment, remember to whom you have come—the Maker of heaven and earth. He is our God. We must submit to His will and authority.

Day 5—Praise the Lord

The LORD appeared to Abram and said, "To your offspring I will give this land. So he built an altar there to the LORD, who had appeared to him."
(Genesis 12:7 NIV)

Abram gave him [the priest Melchizedek] a tenth of everything. (Genesis 14:20 NIV)

David and all Israel were celebrating with all their might before the Lord, with castanets, harps, lyres, timbrels, sistrums and cymbals. (2 Samuel 6:5 NIV)

David was dancing before the Lord with all his might. (2 Samuel 6:14 NIV)

Come let us bow down in worship, let us kneel before the LORD our Maker. (Psalm 95:6 NIV)

"You are worthy, our Lord and God, to receive glory and honor and power, for you created all things, and by your will they were created and have their being." (Revelation 4:11 NIV)

There is much to research and ponder in scripture about worship; the above verses are but a few. As we read these scriptures, we find that we can worship Jesus by making a remembrance of His faithfulness and love. We give Him a portion of our blessings to the church. We can make music, sing, and dance. We can bow down, kneel before Him, and say out loud in prayer that Jesus alone deserves the glory and honor for all He has done.

When we stop to think about what we know of Jesus, what we have experienced with Him and because of Him, the possibilities of worship are endless. Who doesn't love to hear a thank-you from someone? Those simple words have such meaning and depth. Jesus has done much for each of us, much more than we can know this side of heaven. His love is boundless and eternal. Because we see so many references throughout scriptures in the Old and New Testaments, we can conclude that He, like anyone else, appreciates our worship and our thank-yous. In part, Jesus's motivation is His love for us, a love not dependent on our responses. However, with an expression of love back to Him in worship, Jesus is blessed and honored.

How should thanks be expressed? It may be a quiet thank-you, or it may be like David's praise, filled with song, music, and dancing. Are words necessary? I cannot define your form of worship—that is personal and private—but sometimes you don't have the words to express the joy and appreciation in your heart, so take a moment of silence with just you and Him. You can also take advantage of those people who are more expressive or creative than you, and find a song that speaks what you're thinking and feeling. You could also jump to the book of Psalms and use those songs of praise to express your thanks to Jesus.

Making time to praise Jesus draws you closer to Him. You make time to reflect on His character and love, what He means to you, and how He has impacted your life. It is in these times that you draw close to Him, and He, in turn, draws closer to you (James 4:8). Think about what happens when someone in your life takes the time to express love and appreciation toward you. What happens? You are naturally drawn to that person, physically or emotionally, bringing you closer together.

There is a power in praise and rejoicing before our King, the Maker of heaven and earth. In 2 Chronicles 20, we read of an impossible battle won while the nation praised God. It's amazing! Our praise can break down barriers, fill us with joy sought after in sorrow, defeat Satan in his attempt to weaken us, or fill a place with the presence of the Spirit. The possibilities are endless!

Take a moment to worship Jesus and say thank-you to Him right now.

Wrap-Up

Prayer is a response to Jesus. He calls to each of us as a shepherd calls to his sheep. I watched a 2013 video on YouTube that filmed a field of sheep, with spectators trying to use the call the shepherd used to get his sheep to come to him. Each person attempted the call, and the sheep either continued to eat or looked up and then returned to eating. The shepherd then shouted his command to his sheep, and the sheep's response was look up, cry out their collective baa, and come running to him. They move when he moves, stop when he stops, eat and rest when he directs. They learn to trust him and do what he commands. Safety and provision are found in their following and trusting his voice.

In our lives, our reaction to the Shepherd—Jesus—is through prayer. Prayer is a fluid and natural response to the words and movement of Jesus, the great Shepherd. There is no complicated dialogue but a reply born of trust, obedience, and day-to-day life with the Shepherd. We can be silent and simply look up to Him. We can respond to Him by stopping what we are doing at that moment to acknowledge Him or to run plans by Him first to receive guidance and instruction.

As you use the conversation starters I give you each day, my prayer is that you will develop a natural dialogue with Jesus that leads you to recognize His character and voice in your life. This recognition will then lead to a more frequent response to His voice and to experiencing the friendship He longs for with you.

Four

Say, Whaaat?

Memory

First Memory of Prayer

It's challenging to share just one memory regarding my lifelong journey with Jesus, but maybe I should start from the beginning. I was four years old when my parents decided they needed to be part of a church. They loved Jesus and made decisions in life to please Him. This decision to obey included raising their daughter to know of the love of Jesus and to be involved in a church. By the age of seven, I had heard about Jesus every Sunday and regularly in my home for at least three years.

The church of my childhood had regular presentations of the gospel:

"Jesus died on the cross for our sins so that we may be in relationship with Him. Our sin separates us from Him. His death and resurrection paid the penalty for that sin, which can be removed from us for all eternity if we believe. All that is required of us is to believe this truth. John 3:16 tells us, 'For God so loved the world, that he gave his only Son, that whoever believes in him should not perish but have eternal life'" (ESV).

I heard this message over and over again. As a child, I apparently would go to the front of our Sunday school room at church and ask over and over to make this decision of salvation. But it wasn't sinking in. One day at home, with my mom, I got down on my knees in front of our little couch, folded my hands, closed my eyes, and prayed. This prayer was one of my accepting Jesus's salvation for me. I finally realized that this wasn't just a message I heard; it was for me—a message of love and forgiveness.

This first memory of prayer was with a posture of humility and quietness, honoring Jesus and speaking His truth out loud. From that time forward, my communication with Jesus has taken on many forms and has evolved as any deep friendship and relationship evolves.

As with any friend, your prayers will grow and change as you learn to talk with Jesus and recognize His voice and His personality. He is our King and deserves our honor and praise, but His offering of love and relationship allows freedom of expression in our conversations with Him.

Day 1—Father

Our Father, who is in heaven, hallowed be your name. (Matthew 6:9 NIV)

Let's take some time to dive into this prayer that Jesus used to teach about prayer.

Our Father. While on earth, Jesus pointed His listeners to the Father. Over and over again, Jesus brought the Father into the many teachings, prayers, and conversations He had with people. During His last meal with the disciples, Jesus again explained to the disciples that if they saw Him, they had seen the Father (John 13:9–11).

As I've mentioned, prayer is an ongoing conversation with Jesus. When you speak with Him, you are also speaking to the Father, just as John 10:30 points out, in which Jesus declares, "The Father and I are one."

Jesus permits us to address God as Father when He says, "Our Father." Friend, please remember that when you say to Jesus, "Yes, I believe You are the Son of God. You paid the price for my sin by dying on the cross. I believe You rose from the dead," you are a child of God. You have been adopted into His family and are an heir with Jesus. His Father is your Father, and Jesus has given you the ability to call God *Father, Dad*, and even *Daddy*. He is yours, and you are His (John 1:12; Romans 8:16–17). Here, Jesus permits us to address God as Father. There is an intimacy that comes with this title. The Most High God wants to be your Father.

Who is in heaven. Why is the location of God our Father important? Because it reminds us of His authority. When you have an important issue, you want to have access to the person in charge so that you can go to that person with your concern. Here, Jesus is giving you access and permission to talk with the supreme authority and ruler. Our Father not only hears our prayers (Matthew 6:8), but He also has an angel who collects our prayers in golden bowls and places them next to the throne, allowing the Father to breathe them in as incense. Our prayers are precious to Him (Revelation 5:8).

Hallowed be your name. God's name is holy. We may call Him Father, Dad, and even Daddy, but that name is holy and carries authority. He is not a nameless god in an unknown location; He is the Most High God, King of kings, with the supreme authority. Moses was told to take off his shoes while talking with God at the burning bush because he was standing on holy ground. The spirit of God was there with him. Jesus's shed blood has permitted us to be in the presence of the holy God. The privilege of talking with this holy God points out that this very same God seeks to draw us to His amazing love. God has done everything in His power to bring each of us into His presence. Will you allow Jesus to point you to the Father and experience the love He has for you?

Day 2—The Father's Will

> *Your kingdom come, your will be done, on earth as*
> *it is in heaven. (Matthew 6:10 NIV)*

Yesterday we looked at the intimacy Jesus invites us to have with God, the Father. This devotional is intended to help create times and ways to chat with Jesus as a friend. But in this casual, friendly relationship, we cannot lose sight of who Jesus and the Father are—the eternal God. There is always a balance of respect for His authority and an offer of friendship when coming to the Lord. As the Most High God, it is all His kingdom. Father is the Creator, and He reigns over all of it.

Your kingdom come. We pour out our hearts to Him in prayer, but we must also remember that He has a plan. His plan may not be revealed to us in its entirety or in the time we would like it to be made known. We may not even understand as much as we would like to understand, but we must learn to trust Him and His eternal love for each of us (Isaiah 55:8–9; Proverbs 3:5–6; Ephesians 3:17–19; Romans 8:28). This trust comes from experience with Jesus and His Word. Many times, I have sought others who love Jesus and who are more familiar than I am with His ways and love. I needed these people to point me to scriptures about Jesus's character and faithfulness and to pray with me as I attempted to trust Him during difficult or confusing circumstances. Trusting the Lord is not always easy. I like to know the plan and have a clear understanding of my situation. After many years in relationship with Jesus, trusting Him comes more quickly because I can look back on personal memories of His faithfulness to my family and me. These personal memories are my monuments of my encounters with Jesus, just like those made in the Old Testament by Jewish leaders. Jesus and I have a history together.

Your will be done on earth as it is in heaven. How quickly do you think the Lord's words are carried out in heaven? Do you believe there are discussions or refusals? When we utter these words in our prayers to the Lord, we are acknowledging His sovereignty. He is God. I believe this verse means we are agreeing to do His will, trusting that He knows best and has our best interests in mind, even when we don't understand or know what that looks like exactly. Larry Richards, in his book *Every Prayer in the Bible*, says, "Thus, to pray 'your will be done' is both a personal commitment to moral obedience and a commitment to participate in the fulfillment of God's purposes here on earth" (Richards 1998, 140). This too is difficult and tricky. There have been times when I've prayed these words that I've then said, "Not there yet—nope. I think I still want my will to be done and not Yours. Lord, help to want Your will and not my own."

We can say these words in the church as a group of people in worship of Him or just to participate in the event we at the time. But it takes a bit more thought to say these words with full knowledge of Him and the situation you are praying about—at least, it does for me. I can be stubborn and controlling. Letting go of my will to submit to His will is not always fast or easy.

Take a moment to recognize the Lord's authority in your life and your circumstances, not just as a mere subject but as a son or daughter to the Father. Remember His love for you and His offering to help you in all He asks you to do (1 Thessalonians 5:23–24).

Day 3—Daily Needs

> *Give us this day our daily bread. (Matthew 6:11 NIV)*

I am very literal, but is this verse asking us to pray just for our food (or the provision of food) each day? I believe, in part, this is about our provision for our daily food, leading us to regular dependence on Jesus. However, Matthew 6:11 points us to the Old Testament. The Israelites crossed the Red Sea in 1446 BC (The NIV Study Bible - Time Line 1995) (Numbers 16). They wanted food and were complaining about the bounty of food they had left behind in Egypt—where they were slaves. I'm shaking my head as I write this. How often do we long for things that once held us captive?

God's merciful answer to their complaining was to provide quail at night and a sweet, flaky substance that fell from the skies each morning with the dew, called manna. It was versatile and was just enough for each family for every meal. They were to gather twice as much on Friday so that they could observe the Saturday day of rest known as the Sabbath. It was not easy to think that they needed to collect only enough for one day. Those who tried to take more for the next day found maggots in the food in the morning. God was teaching them to trust Him for their daily provision.

We too learn to trust Jesus for our daily provision in whatever form that takes—food, energy, time, emotional strength, and so on. He is a faithful Savior. He is our ever-present help in time of need (Psalm 46:1) and our strong tower (Proverbs 18:10). He will supply all of our needs (Philippians 4:19). No matter how busy our day appears, no matter how much sleep we miss, and no matter what evidence of help we have at the moment, we should come to Him in prayer. We can trust that in some way, we will have what we need for that day. He doesn't always change our circumstances, but He does provide the means to walk through those turbulent times.

As we pray for our daily "bread" or daily provision, we learn to not only pray but to trust and believe. Unfortunately, belief can be difficult, especially under challenging trials, but in the times when faith is difficult, we can cry out, "Lord, help my unbelief." I love that even in those times, He gives us an example that says it's okay to pray, even this prayer found in Mark 9:24. Friend, remember He is gracious and merciful and loves us more than we can understand. Ask Him for your provision for today.

Jesus asks us to pray for our daily bread because He knows

that we need to come to Him for our daily needs. We need to get into the habit of coming to Him each day. This regular chat with Jesus at the beginning of our day will make it easier to go to Him when we face trying days. The regularity of our conversations lead to more and more trust in Him, and trust leads to faith, and faith leads to victory over the difficulty. Oh, what a blessing that is for each of us.

Day 4—Forgiveness

And forgive us our debts, as we also have forgiven
our debtors. (Matthew 6:12 NIV)

I have heard many teachings on forgiveness over the years. The take-away from such lessons might be that our forgiveness from Jesus is dependent on our actions and attitudes. I hope you will dismiss this idea when you look at the character of God, as seen in the entirety of scripture. We read our all-knowing God decided—*before* any portion of creation took place—that He would extend forgiveness to us (Ephesians 1:4–5). God knew how many times each of us would choose our ways over His ways, thus rejecting Him. He created us anyway and planned from the beginning to send Jesus to earth to die for the penalty of our sins. We had *nothing* to do with it. Ephesians 2:8–9 explains this further by stating we are saved from the penalty of sin—eternal death and separation from God—through faith, as a result of the gift from God, not our works or efforts.

This reality brings a new understanding to *forgive us as we have forgiven others.* If our forgiveness is not dependent on our ability and willingness to forgive others, what was Jesus trying to convey? Jesus explains in a couple of parables (Matthew 18:23–34; Luke 7:36–50) that those who know and understand how much they have been forgiven by Him can then extend forgiveness to others. These people have taken the time to see in humility just how much Jesus has forgiven them. When our own sinfulness becomes more apparent, we realize how far from Jesus's holiness and perfection we are. His grace, mercy, and forgiveness become clearer and leave a lasting impression on us. With the revelation of our *own* sinfulness, extending forgiveness to those who have offended us and sinned against us becomes easier and quicker.

This does not mean we need to dwell on our sin or be led to shame, sorrow, and self-loathing. It does mean, however, that we need some careful reflection of our own lives to give us a deeper appreciation and understanding of how loved and forgiven we are by Jesus. This appreciation magnifies His character and shrinks our pride. This humility helps us to extend mercy and forgiveness to those who have wronged us and to glorify Jesus.

It can be hard to face our sin and forget about the person who sinned against us. Our deceitful hearts (Jeremiah 17:9) can mislead us into focusing on others' wrongful acts instead of on Jesus's grace and forgiveness—a revelation that can lead us to confession of our own sin, to a much deeper appreciation of Jesus's love, and to freedom from the hold that sin and shame has on us. Jesus said He did not come into the world to condemn us (John 3:17), so why would we condemn others? We are led to freedom, not bondage or shame, and with that freedom, we can extend that same grace and forgiveness to others.

Day 5—Deliver Us

*And lead us not into temptation, but deliver us
from evil. (Matthew 6:13a KJV)*

"And do not bring us into temptation, but deliver us from the
evil one." Why would Jesus instruct us to pray, "do not bring us
into temptation"? We must again look at the entirety of scripture
for this answer. In 1 Peter 5:8, Satan is described as a lion seeking
whom he might devour. Paul reminds us in 1 Corinthians 10:13
that God is faithful and will not *allow* us to be tempted beyond
what we can endure with Him; He will indeed provide a way out.
Let's not forget Job 1, when Satan comes to heaven for an audience
with God asking to test Job. Jesus even mentions in Luke 22:31–32
that Satan asked to sift Peter like wheat. Jesus Himself had prayed
for Peter that he would not fail, and when Peter turned back from
the sifting, he would strengthen his brothers. All of these verses
point to Satan being the tempter, submissive to the authority of
God. Satan is as dangerous and ravenous as a lion on the prowl,
but he is still subject to God. James 1:13–14 informs us that God
does not lead us into temptation, but by our own evil desires, Satan
can drag us away. In his book *Every Prayer in the Bible*, Larry
Richards points the reader to the word *into* in the above verse,
which in Aramaic means "to succumb to," *not* "led into." We are to
pray that we do not succumb to the temptation of our evil desires,
manipulated by Satan (Richards 1998, 141).

These scriptures inform us that trials and testing will come
our way. Satan, active and alive, will do all he can to come between
us and a relationship with Jesus. We are not alone in this fight.
Jesus gives us this example to pray for help and to ask for the

ability to see the way out provided by the Father. God may allow Satan to test us, but He does not leave us defenseless. He uses this testing to produce endurance, enabling us to become fully mature, lacking nothing (James 1:2–4). Let us not forget how Jesus prayed for Peter in Luke 22:31–32. Romans 8:34 tells us that Jesus is in heaven, interceding for us. He may allow temptation and trials to come our way, but He does not leave us alone and defenseless.

Wrap-Up

For Thine is the kingdom, and the power, and the glory, for ever. Amen. (Matthew 6:13b KJV)

Studying for writing this chapter brought me personal help. My mind tends to wander; I can easily distract myself at any time but especially during prayer. In my frustration with myself, the Spirit reminded me of Jesus's prayer in Matthew 6 and John 17. In each of these prayers, Jesus starts and ends with pointing to the Father's glory and how He sought to bring Him glory, and we too should seek to bring the Father glory. In John 17:1, Jesus begins His prayer by looking toward heaven. In Matthew 6:9, Jesus points us to heaven with His words. Friend, just the remembrance of this action—looking up to the Father—reminded me to literally look up. It is when I did this that I was able to focus my thoughts and finish my prayers that morning.

At the conclusion of this wonderful prayer, let's look at how Jesus points us back to God the Father. He began the prayer with "Our Father, who is in heaven, hallowed be your name," and He now brings us back to whom we are praying. We have looked at many interpretations of these five verses over the last five days. Let's remember that we come before the Father. We should seek to live our lives in such a way that those who encounter us will see that His is the kingdom and the power and the glory forever. Jesus instructs us in Matthew 5:13–16 that we should shine our lights in this dark world and be beacons. We shouldn't hide that light. Shining for Jesus requires prayer and courage, and this too should be a regular part of our chats with Jesus. Living our lives for Jesus is difficult in this world, but it was never meant to be without Jesus's assistance. While sharing your day with Jesus, remember to ask for that help along the way.

Five

Pray without Ceasing (1 Thessalonians 5:17) How Is This Possible?

Memory

Taking time to pray has evolved throughout my life, depending on my season of life and, frankly, how closely I'm in a relationship with Jesus. I understood Jesus's gift of salvation and believed it for myself at the age of seven, so I have comprehended Jesus's presence in my life for most of my life. It's hard to precisely remember my early communication with Jesus or what that looked like on a day-to-day basis. In my childhood church, we had Sunday school, children's church, or the morning service (depending on one's age); Sunday night church; and Wednesday night church or another children's program. In the summer, we had Vacation Bible School and eventually Christian camps in the summer. These were organized and intentional times with Jesus, and the church became my routine as a child.

We talked of Jesus and prayer at home, but I have no memory

of regular time with prayer and/or Bible reading. My first memory of intentional time was in high school, where I learned the disciplines of prayer and Bible study. I tried to maintain these disciplines every day but wasn't always successful. I do remember that prayer was a part of my life; people knew I prayed and relied on me for prayer in their lives.

As I grew—in age and in relationship with Jesus—prayer became more than my Bible-reading time, and I incorporated it into my ordinary day—when I *needed something* for myself or others. I also used songs during times of reflection and thanksgiving of who Jesus is and His love toward me. In my thirties, I learned how to pray without ceasing, as 1 Thessalonians 5:17 instructs. I learned how to keep Christ in the forefront of my mind and include Him and recognize evidence of Him throughout my day, which led to thanksgiving and communication with Him, no matter how mundane or busy my tasks were at the time. I don't pray continually throughout the day, with no other forms of communication, but just like any other person I spend time with, there are sometimes words while working alongside each other and sometimes thoughts of appreciation, coupled with looks or physical touch.

Prayer is not just words but communing alongside Jesus while you do your day-to-day things. I learned to make comments to Jesus while going through my day. I became more mindful of those thoughts that popped into my mind as I worked. Relaxed conversation with Jesus on my part allowed me to recognize His friendly communication with me. Praying without ceasing is not literal; for me, it's more of a mindful awareness of Jesus's presence in my life. The prayers throughout my day can be extended intercession for myself or others—a quick word, an "I love you," a cry for help, or relaxed chatter. It varies moment by moment and day by day, as in other intimate relationships in my life.

Day 1—Are You Praying for His Glory or Yours?

And when you pray, you must not be like the hypocrites. For they love to stand and pray in the synagogues and at the street corners, that they may be seen by others. Truly, I say to you; they have received their reward. But when you pray, go into your room and shut the door and pray to your Father who is in secret. And your Father who sees in secret will reward you. (Matthew 6:5–6 ESV)

If you were to open the Bible to Matthew 6 and read what Jesus says about giving, prayer, and fasting, you'd see He uses the word *when*. Jesus isn't instructing us to do these things; He assumes that we already have made giving, prayer, and fasting part of our regular worship and obedience to Him. I think this is a key understanding of prayer. It's not an *if* but a *when*. Jesus doesn't get into the time we pray in this passage; He addresses it as if it's already happening.

The common practice of the Pharisees was to pray on the street corner and in the synagogue or temple to garner attention and admiration. It is appropriate to pray in public; Jesus did this many times in scripture. Jesus cautions us to check the reason we are publicly praying. If it is for your own attention and praise, you have received your reward. If you are praying in public as a witness of your faith or to be a comfort to someone, then your motivation likely is selfless.

Jesus instructs us to make it our habit to pray in private. He knew the value of one-on-one time with the Father—no distractions or obligations, just prayer with the Father. Psalm 46:10 tells us, "Be still and know that I am God." When we are alone in our prayer times, we are able to be still, hear the Spirit that responds to us, and learn who Jesus is. It's no different from having one-on-one time with someone special. Hanging out with friends or family is great, but when you have just that one person with you, your attention is undivided and precious. Pray in private, and create those valuable times with Jesus.

Have you ever done a systems check on your device or car? Things may appear to be functioning just fine, but a systems check will identify a hidden issue that needs to be addressed to avoid a problem down the road. Having an appropriately motivated heart will help you to avoid a sin issue down the road. Do a heart check; ask yourself what motivates you to pray. What keeps you from praying out loud or motivates you to be the first person to pray in a group setting?

Day 2—Prayer Ideas

> But Jesus often withdrew to lonely places and prayed. (Luke 5:16 NIV)

When I did a word search on "prayer" on BibleGateway.com, I read that Jesus

- offered prayer after being baptized (Luke 3:21),
- prayed before some of the meals He participated in (Luke 22:17; 24:30),
- prayed before the miracle of the feeding of the 5000 (Matthew 14:19),
- gave thanks to the Father (Luke 10:21; John 11:41),
- petitioned the Father to forgive (Luke 23:34),
- prayed after the death of His cousin, John the Baptist (Matthew 14:23),
- prayed to glorify the Father (John 17:1),
- prayed for the disciples and those who would become His followers from the testimonies of the disciples (John 17),
- prayed in the His time of need in the garden of Gethsemane (Matthew 26:36–46), and
- prayed right before He died (Luke 23:46).

In these few verses about Jesus's prayer life, we see that we should do the following:

- Go alone to pray.
- Pray with and for others.
- Give thanks.
- Pray while grieving.
- Pray in difficult times.
- Pray to bless food.
- Pray for ourselves in difficult times.
- Pray to glorify God.
- Surrender to God's plan.
- Ask for forgiveness for ourselves and others.
- Pray during spiritual growth and changes in our lives.

We witness in Jesus's life that we should pray often and include God in the little things as well as the big things. His love for each of us is vast, and He wants to be a part of our lives.

Some of my little things include what will be comfortable to wear to work on a given day. Jesus knows what the day will be like late in the day, and He can advise me on my choices. Which route is best to take while driving? Again, He knows what lies ahead and can give me good advice. What should I make for dinner? This often is a difficult decision, depending on how many will be having dinner and who I'm feeding.

The "big things" in which you should include God—the important prayer topics—are, no doubt, easy for you to figure out without my prompting you.

Take a moment to think, and ask Jesus why you pray or don't pray. What keeps you from engaging in regular conversation with Jesus?

Day 3—Praying Morning and Night

> *Only be strong and very courageous, being careful to do according to all the law that Moses my servant commanded you. Do not turn from it to the right hand or to the left, that you may have good success wherever you go. This Book of the Law shall not depart from your mouth, but you shall meditate on it day and night, so that you may be careful to do according to all that is written in it. For then you will make your way prosperous, and then you will have good success. (Joshua 1:7–8 ESV)*

Joshua was Moses's protege while the Israelites wandered in the desert for forty years. Joshua was strong and courageous. He was one of the spies who went into the Promised Land forty years before the above verses. He and Caleb were the only two spies who saw the blessings of the Promised Land and were not afraid of the strength and might of the people in that land.

But now, Moses has died, and Joshua is left to lead the people of Israel into Canaan to conquer, defeat the people, and inhabit the land. The people he leads often turn their backs on the Lord and are challenging to lead. Before going into the land and battle, the Lord speaks the above words to Joshua. God knows what lies ahead. He knows Joshua's heart and knows what will give Joshua the strength and courage he needs. Joshua must know the scriptures, and he must meditate on them day and night. Meditation is contemplation.

The Lord doesn't say to read the scriptures every morning and night merely to think about them. We are to let them be a part of our thoughts and minds. This practice brings wisdom and strength at the beginning of the day and peace and rest at the end of the day. Meditation leads to memorization and a more in-depth understanding.

When you fight battles, the words of God will be fresh in your mind. Unlike Joshua, many of us will not face physical combat, but Paul tells in Ephesians 6:12, "We do not fight against flesh and blood but the rulers, authorities, and powers of darkness in the heavenly places." First Peter 5:7 tells us, "Satan prowls around like a roaring lion, seeking whom he might devour." Jesus showed us that while being tempted (Matthew 4:1–11), the way to defeat Satan is to remember the words of God correctly.

Going back to Ephesians 6, we learn that the sword of the Spirit is the Word of God. While we go about our days, we include Jesus in our lives and pray to Him often. It is during these prayers to Him that we pray the words of the Bible to fight temptations and to strengthen us during our battles. In the morning, meditate on the Word of God, pray to Him for strength and courage to face your day, and be victorious. In the evening, give Jesus thanks for the assistance He gave that day and the victories won, and lay those things not yet resolved at His feet, finding rest and peace.

How about now? Are you planning your day or ending it?

Day 4—Pray Regularly

When Daniel knew that the document had been signed, he went to his house where he had windows in his upper chamber open toward Jerusalem. He got down on his knees three times a day and prayed and gave thanks before his God, as he had done previously. (Daniel 6:10 ESV)

When you read the book of Daniel and learn who he was and what kind of man he chose to be, you will find discipline and the strength to choose obedience to God over the temptation to please men and remain safe. Daniel makes choices to be disciplined and is not afraid to show people this discipline, which allows him to endure slavery and captivity in the Babylonian Empire. Daniel's devotion to God did not spare him captivity in Babylon, but that discipline allowed him to find strength and wisdom that led to respect and eventually power within the empire that had enslaved him.

Our devotion does not always remove us from trouble or seemingly impossible situations, but it does give us the power and strength to endure the situations and find victory in the midst of them.

In these verses, Daniel chooses to go somewhere alone to pray, and he does it three times per day, as per the Jewish custom of praying every morning, afternoon, and evening. Again, despite Daniel's circumstances, he chooses to remain faithful to God and the customs he has learned. Daniel exercises discipline and obedience.

I am not suggesting that we have to pray every morning, afternoon, and evening, but with discipline, we should make prayer a regular part of our lives. Having a specific time to pray and praying alone allows prayer to be uninterrupted (for the most part) and to become a part of our lives. I also recommend that this commitment to prayer be a part of our lives no matter what our circumstances. We see here and throughout scripture that obedience to Jesus does not ensure a life without turmoil, but it does ensure that we will have the strength, peace, and wisdom to endure the trials of life with victory. Our victory may not be a change in our circumstances, but it will be our ability to rise above our circumstances and remain in obedience to Jesus, while being a light in the darkness as He calls us to be for Him and those living life with us.

Friend, how you can make prayer a regular part of your day throughout the day?

Day 5

Pray without ceasing. (1 Thessalonians 5:17 KJV)

I've mentioned that prayer evolved into an everyday practice as I intentionally made prayer a part of my day-to-day life. Of course, I don't pray every minute of every day. My mind is too vulnerable to distraction, which is why part of my prayer practice is journaling to keep my mind focused. I try to do all to the glory of God, as Paul instructs in 1 Corinthians 10:31, but that too is a goal, not a perfected practice.

I came across the method of incorporating the continual conversation or awareness of Christ in my life after reading the book *The Practice of the Presence of God*, written by Brother Lawrence, a seventeenth-century monk. As a layman, he suffered injuries during his service in the French army; after that, he became a monk in the Discalced Carmelite monastery in Paris.

Brother Lawrence worked in the kitchen during his days in the monastery. He wasn't one of the teaching monks, but those in his order came to respect him for his attitude and devotion to God, no matter what he was doing. After his death, his maxims were found. He had granted four interviews to the Abbe de Beaufort. These are what make up the content of his book (Christianity Today n.d.).

This book gave me practical ways to keep Jesus at the forefront of my mind, thereby including Him in my everyday life. This intentional remembering is what makes regular conversation and praise to Jesus possible. It also helps me to realize there is nothing too small, boring, or mundane in my life for Jesus not to be a part of it, not because He's particularly interested in that particular thing or event but because He is interested in and in love with me.

Do you understand? Jesus is genuinely in love with you, and every part of your life is significant to Him. Do you believe this truth? Talk with Him about it. He's waiting right here to hear from you.

Wrap-Up

You have seen many examples of real times of prayer and for which events in your life you should pray—there is much to contemplate and pray about! If you're still not sure what to say, ask Jesus. He knows your life and the season you find yourself in right now. Jesus says, "He did not come here to condemn you but save you" (John 3:17 ESV). He tells us in John 10:10 that He came to bring us abundant life. The literal definition of "abundant" is *wow*! He wants you to go to Him and be wowed. Soak all this information in and think about it. Then turn to Jesus in prayer to find out what you will take away right now. What will become your prayer discipline right now?

I have had different seasons of prayer in my life. While I was trying to become disciplined, I chose a time and stuck to it. I stumbled but started again. In other seasons, I had more time and would spend long periods alone in prayer and meditation. I found Jesus in these times and found the friend He is to me. We have had private and personal moments that I cherish.

Then I've had seasons when I missed those long times alone and felt guilty because I couldn't figure out how to fit in the hours I'd had in the previous season of life. It was here that Jesus gave me mercy and grace and removed the shame I had put on myself.

Jesus helped me to understand that the start of my day would sometimes be only a *hello*. Other mornings would be a prayer; another day, prayer and Bible study; another, intercessory prayer for others. Each day looked different, and that was okay because that was how my time needed to be in that period of my life. The point was to make time for Jesus, even if it looked different every day. I made time for Him and included Him in many moments of the day. It was here that I found rest, peace, and freedom. I found a companion in the busyness of that time. That was a season, and then a new one arose, which began another adjustment and commitment in my prayer and Bible study time with Jesus. As with any relationship in life, there is an ebb and flow, up and downs, busyness and calm. You just make it work.

Jesus wants to be a part of our everyday lives. He's not demanding, but He is the King of kings. He deserves our respect, honor, and obedience. He also wants to be our friend and be included in our lives, which change with many different seasons— He'll go with the flow. Ask Him and let Him guide you to discipline and a deeper relationship with Him.

Six

Jesus's Prayer Before the Garden (John 17)

Memory

In this chapter we will look carefully at Jesus's final recorded prayer before His arrest—a prayer He says aloud for the disciples to hear. He is transparent, and He was focused on others before His horrific and imminent death. It is incredible to me.

I had more time to finish this devotional than I'd expected because I fell on a wet floor and broke my kneecap into two pieces, which definitely was not in my plan. I was in an immobilizer for eight weeks, followed by more than six weeks of physical therapy, much of which occurred while I was off work. In the days before surgery, as my husband and I tried to wrap our heads around yet another knee surgery and the unknowns of recovery, I did not spend prayer time thinking of others and eloquently speaking of the love I have for Jesus and His plans. I was scared. What would they find during the surgery? Were any tendons or ligaments damaged? Was the kneecap only in two pieces, as the x-ray indicated? How would I care for myself, and who would help me? There was much uncertainty, fear, and anxiety.

Thankfully, these thoughts weren't all-consuming. My husband and I are planners and problem solvers, and we worked with the information we had at the time. My prayers, however, were filled with verses on trusting Jesus and His plans and not leaning on my own understanding. The day before my surgery, the daily verse was from Isaiah 41:10—"Don't be afraid for I am with you. Don't be discouraged for I am your God." I was reminded that I was genuinely afraid. I am not a fearful person or even an anxious person, but these emotions were difficult to manage.

Jesus is faithful, and verse after verse reminded me, "I can because of I AM." Jesus was refocusing my thoughts on Him. Amid my uncertainty, I could stand.

This experience brought blessings and evidence of Jesus's provision, love, and mercy. It also made me appreciate this prayer even more because my head and my prayers were not focused on others in the days leading to my surgery. How amazing is He and His love toward each of us?

Day 1—Glorifying the Father

> When Jesus had spoken these words, he lifted up his eyes to heaven, and said, "Father, the hour has come; glorify your Son that the Son may glorify you, since you have given him authority over all flesh, to give eternal life to all whom you have given him. And this is eternal life, that they know you, the only true God, and Jesus Christ whom you have

sent. I glorified you on earth, having accomplished the work that you gave me to do. And now, Father, glorify me in your own presence with the glory that I had with you before the world existed." (John 17:1-5 ESV)

We read of Jesus praying throughout the New Testament, but here, we have His words to the Father right before He entered the garden of Gethsemane and eventually was arrested. He had a personal moment with the Father in front of the disciples after their last meal together.

Let's get in the moment here. Jesus knows that arrest and crucifixion await Him. He knows this is the last time He will be alone with the disciples before His death. The carefully orchestrated evening will benefit the disciples. Jesus knows that great suffering is coming their way. What does He do? He includes them in His prayer to His Father. He demonstrates prayer to them.

We first read that Jesus acknowledges the Father. He looks up and addresses Him by name—"Father." We are not always at liberty to look up while praying, especially if we're driving at the time, but we can acknowledge Him by name. *Father* is sometimes a tricky word because it may be associated with negative feelings about our fathers. *Father* can also seem very formal. Call Him by the name that is most comfortable for you. If "Father" is uncomfortable or painful for you now, you can address Jesus. After all, Jesus tells us in John 10:30 that He and the Father are One.

Jesus then pours out the deepest desire of His heart to glorify the Father. His whole life on earth has been spent loving the Father and others. He has done everything the Father has asked so that all may see the Father. Jesus has accomplished this by completing the work the Father gave Him to do here on earth. Jesus brought attention and honor to the Father through His obedience (glorifying Him).

Jesus concludes this portion of the prayer and speaks of what He longs for in this moment—to be in the presence of the Father again with nothing muting that experience. He loves the Father and yearns to be in His presence.

This may not be an exchange any of us has with God, but just think about it. Doesn't it feel amazing when those who are important to you make an extra effort to express their deep love and appreciation for you? God is no different. Whether you feel more comfortable using the name Jesus or Father, take a moment to express how it would be to stand in His presence and see Him face-to-face.

Day 2—Prayers for the Disciples

I have manifested your name to the people whom you gave me out of the world. Yours they were, and you gave them to me, and they have kept your word. Now they know that everything that you have given me is from you. For I have given them the words that you gave me, and they have received them and have come to know in truth that I came from you; and they have believed that you sent me. I am praying for them. I am not praying for the world but for those whom you have given me, for they are yours. All mine are yours, and yours are mine, and I am glorified in them. And I am no longer in the world, but they are in the world, and I am coming to you. Holy Father, keep them in your name, which you have given me, that they may be one, even as we are one. While I was with them, I kept them in your name, which you have given me. I have guarded them, and not one of them has been lost except the son of destruction, that the Scripture might be fulfilled. But now I am coming to you, and these things I speak in the world, that they may have my joy fulfilled in themselves. I have given them your word, and the world has hated them because they are not of the world, just as I am not of the world. I do not ask that you take them out of the world, but that you keep them from the evil one. They are not of the world, just as I am not of the world. Sanctify them in the truth; your word is truth. As you sent me into the world, so I have sent them into the world. And for their sake I consecrate myself, that they also may be sanctified in truth. (John 17:6–19 ESV)

Now we read that Jesus is praying for His disciples. He knows that He will no longer be on earth, living with them physically. He surrenders Himself into the capable and loving hands of the Father. Have you had moments like this? Have you ever asked someone who loves you to pray for you, and that person takes a moment to pray for you aloud right there? It is such a blessing.

Jesus testifies to the character of these men to the Father in prayer. Ponder this for a moment. These men have finally put it together that Jesus and the Father are one. They are beginning to grasp that His death is coming. What does Jesus do? He acknowledges and affirms them and their belief to the Father in prayer.

Later, this moment and these words will have such meaning and strength for these same disciples, who will be persecuted and eventually killed for their faith in Jesus Christ.

Jesus knows that they will be persecuted for their faith and obedience. He doesn't ask the Father to remove them from this persecution but to fill them with joy and to sanctify—make them holy—through the scriptures. Jesus acknowledges that the Word of God is truth and has the power to make these men holy. He also states that what He will consecrate Himself for their sake.

These are powerful words for the disciples, but what of us? How does this particular passage apply to our prayers? James tells us that the prayers of a righteous man accomplish much. Paul describes the Word of God as the sword of the Spirit. When we pray to the Lord, it is useful and powerful to speak back His truth in prayer. When you pray for yourself or someone who is suffering trials, the natural reaction is to ask God to remove you or the other person from that circumstance to avoid pain and suffering. But that, unfortunately, is not always God's plan.

As you follow Jesus's example, ask the Lord to fill that person or you with joy and to help you or another find strength and holiness in the Word of God. Why the Word, and why holiness? Jesus calls us to be His light in the world, bringing others to a saving knowledge of Him. James tells us that we suffer, which allows us to bring comfort and compassion to others who suffer.

We cannot know the ways of the Father (Isaiah 55:8–9), but we know that He provides strength, hope, love, and peace in our times of need. We also know that He does not waste suffering. The people who suffer and know Jesus can share what they have received in their times of suffering to bring that same joy, peace, and hope to others in their suffering. Go ahead, and—in mercy—pray for someone's deliverance, but also pray for him or her while that person is in the trial.

Day 3

I do not ask for these only, but also for those who will believe in me through their word, that they may all be one, just as you, Father, are in me, and I in you, that they also may be in us, so that the world may believe that you have sent me. (John 17:20–21 ESV)

Here we read of Jesus's prayer for us. Yes, Jesus prayed for each of us at the Last Supper. He cares for and is thankful for those who came to believe in Him without having to see Him first (John 20:29). This message began when the eleven spread the message of salvation after Jesus gave them the great commission, found in Matthew 28:16–20. Jesus knew that His disciples would find courage and strength and spread His message of salvation and hope to all the world. He also knew that those who heard their news would, in turn, spread that same message, on and on and on until today, when we read again of Jesus's love for us and foreknowledge of our love for Him.

Jesus prayed for you and me.

How amazing is this man, friend, God? Can we truly fathom the depth, height, width, or length of His love for us?

What was His prayer for us at that moment and even now? He wanted us to be one with Him and the Father. He wanted this oneness, this unity, with the Triune God to be evident and extended to other believers, the church of Jesus. He wanted unity for all followers of Jesus, unity that brings us closer to Him and then displays His glory to all of those around us.

This oneness and unity are what draws others to Jesus and what He has to offer us. A genuine relationship with Him is made possible by His death and resurrection, which paid the penalty for our sins. Nothing more stands in the way of real and eternal life with Him.

Day 4—Unity of Believers

> *The glory that you have given me I have given to them, that they may be one even as we are one, I in them and you in me, that they may become perfectly one, so that the world may know that you sent me and loved them even as you loved me. (John 17:22–23 ESV)*

In his book *When God Prays*, pastor and author Skip Heitzig notes, "In other words, a unified church will convince people that there is a God in heaven" (Heitzig 2003, 116). He further says, "Although neither uniformity nor organizational consistency equates with true Christian unity, we can't overemphasize the importance of fellowship with other Christians. I need you, and you need me. This issue is unity of heart, spirit and purpose—it's more internal than external" (Heitzig 2003, 132).

We know that we have passed out of death into life, because we love the brothers. (1 John 3:14 ESV)

What do all these words say to us as Christ-followers today? Jesus wants us to experience true love and oneness with the Triune God for our sakes and for those who would find Him through us and our unity. We can talk of scriptures and things going on at our respective churches, but if those with whom we walk through life don't see unity and love with God and other followers of Jesus, we've missed the mark. When you read the Bible, you will see how Christ embodied perfection in all that He did here on earth. He loved thoroughly and sacrificially, first to His Father and then to everyone He met. He didn't tolerate sin, but He loved each and every sinner. He didn't come to condemn but to enlighten and to draw others to the love of the Father.

Jesus told His followers that He did not come into the world to condemn the world but to save it through His death and resurrection. Jesus is God, yet He did not condemn or judge. Who are we to do otherwise? We, like Jesus, must extend servant-like love that leads people to the truth of the gospel message and to a relationship with Jesus, the Father, and the Spirit. We must ask ourselves if our motivation for actions, feelings, and words is from pride and being right or from selfless love to lead others to Jesus's love? This is not always easy to remember in the moment, especially if we know what scripture is saying, and our belief is right.

We must hold (Ephesian 4:2–10; 1 Peter 3:15) to the truths of the Bible, just as Paul and then Peter instructed us. We must speak that truth and answer questions with gentleness. We read our Bible, learning of Jesus and His character. We pray and get to know Him more intimately. His character is seen in us, bringing Him glory, just as He brought honor to the Father. That oneness with Jesus extends to other Christ-followers who demonstrate true love and unity to those separate from Christ, that each of them may know Jesus's love and salvation.

Day 5

Father, I desire that they also, whom you have given me, may be with me where I am, to see my glory that you have given me because you loved me before the foundation of the world. O righteous Father, even though the world does not know you, I know you, and these know that you have sent me. I made known to them your name, and I will continue to make it known, that the love with which you have loved me may be in them, and I in them. (John 17:24–26 ESV)

What a conclusion to His prayer! Jesus begins His prayer with love and honor toward the Father. This has been His motivation for obedience His entire life. As you take the time to read through the Gospels—Matthew, Mark, Luke, and John—you will witness how Jesus's brothers and sisters rejected Him. His village rejected Him. Israelites rejected Him because of His hometown of Nazareth. Religious leaders and even two of the disciples rejected Him. This was not a man motivated by popularity and acceptance. He did not suffer from people-pleasing.

Jesus is a man driven by love—love for His Father and love for the people He came to save.

I can't help wondering if, in this prayer, Jesus is reminding Himself of the longing of His heart, encouraging Himself and refocusing His heart because He knows what is coming next. He knows where Judas is and that His own arrest is imminent. His desire is for us to be with Him in heaven. This is why He came to earth—to make a way for us to be in a relationship with Him and to eventually be in heaven with Him (John 14:3).

Jesus is God, and He was a man at the same time. His actual glorified body was hidden from His friends, and He longed to be known and revealed to them, with nothing in the way of their vision and understanding.

How precious is that? The God of the universe, the Maker of heaven and earth, longs for each of us to know Him, to share His heavenly home with us, and to introduce us to His Father. These are the words of a true bridegroom. What a picture of His love for us.

Sit in this revelation of Jesus's love for a few moments. This is real and complete love and a longing for each of us. These are the final words of His prayer. Thank Jesus for the love He showed in the verse and continues to show us, day after day.

Wrap-Up

The last time Jesus spoke with the remaining eleven disciples was when they were in the upper room where they celebrated their last Passover meal together. Imagine leaving your family, your very close friends, your small group that traveled everywhere with you for over three years, those you have mentored and trained. These are the ones Jesus was leaving behind. These words are precious.

We can see the love Jesus displays in this prayer. These are His men—the men the Father gave Him to impart His heart and love for the Father. Jesus poured Himself into these men for over three years. He loved them deeply! See this as you read; see the love Jesus had for them. Notice, however, how He started this prayer—with His love for the Father. I can't help but remember 1 John 1:7—"Walk in the light, as He is in the light, we have fellowship with one another" (ESV). This was what Jesus was modeling and praying for His precious friends.

Jesus walks with the Father and the Spirit. They live in perfect harmony, a oneness that defines who They are. They are in tune and operate in complete love. They are one. Jesus displays this in His prayer. He starts by honoring the Father and loving Him, first and foremost. Then His prayer moves to His disciples, interceding on their behalf with His Dad. He knows that these men will be obedient to the calling given to them. He knows that one day, His future followers will read of this encounter, this precious and intimate prayer.

Jesus knows that we—the future followers—need prayer and evidence of His intercession for us. He also knows that this prayer for the followers to come will spur on His disciples to obedience because if these future believers are valued enough for Jesus to pray about them in His last days, then this will be important to the disciples when they are faced with the decision to be obedient or disobedient.

Can you imagine the moments when the disciples were faced with horrific deaths; when they were asked to deny Jesus or die for Him? Where did their strength and determination come from? I believe, in part, these words in Jesus's last prayer strengthened them and inspired them to obedience. "Yes, Jesus! My life and my sacrifice are not for naught! My actions and teachings will be remembered and spoken again, allowing more to find You and become sons and daughters of the Most High God! Will I stand for Jesus and die today? Yes, I stand! Yes, I die! Because I want more to come to the knowledge of you, I want more to know and live for You."

These are the last words He leaves with His disciples that are specifically for them—a prayer from the heart for them that will last forever more. He is leaving, but He does not forget them or abandon them. He is, in this passage, interceding on their behalf and our behalf, as He will continue to do while in heaven. This prayer is one of the last intimately spoken and transcribed moments Jesus had with His men—and ultimately, with us.

He took the time to pray for us! Thousands of years after Christ prayed for us, we can find hope, love, and strength to stand firm in our faith. He loves us that much. The Holy Spirit, through the will of the Father, took the time to make sure that John remembered and wrote down this moment for the Christians. He wrote encouragement to and for us, all these years later. We are deeply loved by the Father, the Son, and the Holy Spirit.

Works Cited

Behind the Name. 2019. *Behind the Name.* June 13. Accessed 2019. www.behindthename.com/name/Jacob.

Bible Study Tools. 2019. *Bible Study Tools.* www.biblestudytools. com/commentaries/revelation/related-topics/samaritans. html.

Christian Stack Exchange. 2013. *Christian Stack Exchange.* April. Accessed August 2019. www.christianity.stackexchange.com/ questions/15586/reason-for-drawing-water-at-unusual-time.

Christianity Today. n.d. *Christianity Today.* Accessed 2019. www. christianitytoday.com/history/people/innertravelers/brother-lawrence.html.

Darby, John N. 1970. *Synopsis of the Books of the Bible Volume 1.* Winschoten, Netherlands: H. L. Heijkoop.

Got Questions. 2019. *Got Questions .* July. Accessed 2019. www. gotquestions.org/amp/God-of-Abraham-Isaac-Jacob.html.

—. 2019. *Got Questions.* July. Accessed 2019. https://www. gotquestions.org/Saul-of-Tarsus.html.

Heitzig, Skip. 2003. *When God Prays* . Wheaton, IL: Tyndale House Publishing, Inc.

Institute in Basic LIfe Principles. n.d. *Institute in Basic Life Principles.* Accessed 20189. https://iblp.org/questions/what-significance-using-different-postures-prayer.

1999, 2003. *Judeo-Christian Research.* Accessed 2019. www.juchre. org/articles/fig.htm.

LaPort, Brian. 2013. *Archives Near Emmaus.* April 26. Accessed 2019. www.nearemmaus.wordpress.com/2013/04/26/paul-the-zealot/.

Lawrence, Brother. 2016. *The Practice of the Presence of God.* Eastford, CT: Martino Fine Books.

Merriam-Webster. June. *Merriam-Webster Dictionary.* 2019: Merriam-Webster.

Richards, Larry. 1998. *Every Prayer in the Bible: Discover God's Patterns for Effective Prayer.* Nashville, TN: Thomas Nelson Publishing.

Stanley, Andy. 2012. *Free.* October - November. Accessed July 2019. www.wecanbefree.org.

1995. *The NIV Study Bible - Time Line.* Grand Rapids, MI: Zondervan Publishing House.

2013. *YouTube.* November 17. Accessed 2019. www.youtube.com/ watch?v=e45dVgWgV64&t=29s.

CPSIA information can be obtained
at www.ICGtesting.com
Printed in the USA
BVHW031054090120
569086BV00001B/108/P

9 781973 681199